IN PRAISE OF
indecency

IN PRAISE OF
indecency

THE LEADING INVESTIGATIVE
SATIRIST SOUNDS OFF ON HYPOCRISY, CENSORSHIP
AND FREE EXPRESSION

BY PAUL KRASSNER

CLEIS
PRESS

For Margo St. James,
who continues to serve on the front lines
of the Women's Liberation Movement

Published in the United States by Cleis Press Inc., P.O. Box 14697, San Francisco, California 94114. Printed in Canada.

Cover design: Scott Idleman
Cover photograph: Alfred Gescheidt/Getty Images
Text design: Frank Wiedemann
Cleis logo art: Juana Alicia
10 9 8 7 6 5 4 3 2 1

Library of Congress Cataloging-in-Publication Data

Krassner, Paul.
In praise of indecency / Paul Krassner.
    p. cm.
ISBN 978-1-57344-350-0 (pbk. : alk. paper)
1. Satire, American. I. Title.

PS3561.R286I5 2009
814'.54--dc22

                              2009006703

CONTENTS

SUSIE BRIGHT
INTERVIEWS PAUL KRASSNER

SUSIE BRIGHT INTERVIEWS PAUL KRASSNER

Susie: Paul, what's the story of the first "dirty picture" you ever saw?

Paul: When I was eleven or twelve, my older brother, George, had somehow obtained nude photos of movie stars, like Rita Hayworth and Burt Lancaster.

"What are these for?" I asked.

"To give you a hard-on," he replied.

And so we started selling them for 75 cents each. Our parents never knew. In retrospect, it seems like destiny that I ended up writing a column, "One Hand Jerking," for *AVN* (Adult Video News) *Online*—a slick magazine that serves as a trade journal for the vast, lucrative Internet porn industry—where the content of *In Praise of Indecency* originally appeared.

Also in junior high school, my classmates were passing

around these little three inches high by four inches wide anonymous, underground, eight-page comics, known as "fuck books," consisting of comic-strip characters, famous actors, sports heroes, political figures, traveling salesmen and notorious criminals—all having sex, accompanied by vulgar speech balloons.

In 1997, Simon & Schuster published *Tijuana Bibles: Art and Wit in America's Forbidden Funnies, 1930s-1950s*. In an introductory essay, Pulitzer Prize-winning author Art Spiegelman wrote: "... This sort of psycho-sociological analysis is important, but inevitably sounds like a defensive ploy to inject Socially Redeeming Value into the concupiscent stew. Paul Krassner, editor of *The Realist* and, briefly, *Hustler,* aptly insisted that 'appealing to the prurient interest *is* a socially redeeming value.'"

Susie: You were a child prodigy at the violin... was there any erotic aspect to playing the strings, or learning that discipline, obvious or not so obvious?

Paul: I began playing the violin when I was three years old, practiced myself right out of my childhood, and didn't really wake up to my own existence until I was six, onstage, playing the "Vivaldi Concerto in A Minor," in the process of becoming the youngest concert artist ever to perform at Carnegie Hall. There was nothing erotic about it.

However, the next year, I saw my first movie, *Intermezzo.* It was also Ingrid Bergman's first movie. She fell in love with her violin teacher, and I fell in love with the background-music theme, the song "Intermezzo." I couldn't fathom why it *just felt so good* to hear this specific combination of notes in a certain order with a particular rhythm, but it gave me such pleasure to keep humming that sweet melody over and over to myself. It was like having a secret companion. Now *that* was an erotic experience, not to my genitals but to the depths of my soul. I couldn't wait to tell my violin teacher that I wanted to learn how to play "Intermezzo." But he obviously didn't share my enthusiasm. "'Intermezzo?'" he sneered. "That's not right for you."

His words reverberated in my heart. *That's not right for you!* How could he know what was right for *me*? This wasn't merely a turndown of my request. It was a universal declaration of war upon the individual.

Susie: So many people have a *Deep Throat* or Linda Lovelace story. I washed her car, for a few bucks, parked up the street, when I was in high school. My first acid trip coincided with seeing her introduce Deep Purple at a monster rock fest on a desert racetrack…. What's yours?

Paul: Deep Throat inspired me to write a little book—*Tales of Tongue Fu*, a New Age media satire about a man with a 15-inch tongue—which has just been republished. In this fable, Tongue Fu sees the movie and considers Linda Lovelace to be his soul mate because her clitoris is in her throat.

Susie: And really… have you ever been in a porn film?

Paul: No, not that I know of… unless, of course, there was a hidden camera in the room.

Susie: What is the best drug, in your experience, to accompany sex? The worst? I asked a group of older folks once, about their favorite combo, and they said: pot and espresso.

Paul: The best enhancer has always been marijuana, combined with LSD, and later on a terrific aphrodisiac called MDA—which would have been distributed in America by one of Charles Manson's victims—and, more recently, good old Ecstasy. I was once going to be in a threesome with two ex-girlfriends, but we had all ingested Quaaludes and fell asleep. That turned out to be the worst.

Susie: Are you jealous, or have you been attracted to jealous lovers? What is your masochism tango on the monogamy question?

Paul: As for jealousy, I only experienced it when I felt insecure in a relationship. And I was distracted by jealous lovers who kept needing reassurance. As for "masochism tango," well, that's a loaded question. I'm totally pro-choice about abortion rights, drug use, ice-cream flavors and sexual practices. So, in my life, there have been times when I've enjoyed promiscuity, other times when I've enjoyed celibacy, and currently I'm enjoying monogamy with my wife, Nancy, not because of any wedding vows we took—obviously, marital vow-taking has never prevented adultery—but rather because it's my choice.

Susie: When you were a kid, who did you think were the "sexiest" stars?

Paul: Ann Sheridan was an actress who became my first fantasy babe.

Susie: How did that change, or not, as you grew up?

Paul: Later it was Brigitte Bardot. And the latest was Halle Berry.

Susie: Women often say, when asked why they were attracted to a man, that "he was funny, he made me laugh." Not so many men would answer that way when asked about a woman's appeal. What do you make of that?

Paul: Well, virtually every man I know is attracted by a woman's sense of humor. Personally, I find it almost inextricable from physical attraction. Occasionally, in fact, when a woman has made me laugh, I've actually gotten an erection.

Susie: Did you ever give your daughter sexual or romantic advice? What was the result?

Paul: Her mother, Jeanne, took care of all that stuff. A few years after our marriage broke up, when Holly was seven, I moved from New York to San Francisco. We stayed in touch by mail and phone, she would stay with me on her school vacations, and I would come to New York a few times every year. She came to live with me for a whole year when she was eleven, accompanied me on a shamans and healers trek in Ecuador when she was fifteen, and lived with me again for a few years when she was seventeen.

When Holly was ten, on one of my trips to New York, I took her and Jeanne out for dinner.

"Mommy told me all about sex," she confided in the restaurant.

"Oh, really? What did you learn?"

"Oh, she told me about orgasms and blow jobs."

I blushed. They laughed.

One evening, when she was sixteen, Holly called me. "Hold on a second," she said, then held her phone to the speaker of her stereo, and I heard Carly Simon singing, "Daddy, I'm no virgin, and I've already waited too long...." Then Holly hung up quickly. I began to laugh and cry simultaneously. I was laughing at the creative way she had chosen to share this news—my generation had avoided communicating with parents about sex altogether—and I guess maybe I was crying because I never got any when *I* was sixteen. The sexual revolution had still been just a horny dream back then. Now I was delighted to see its legacy in action, yet I also felt a certain vestigial resentment. "Why, these young kids today, they just don't appreciate the joy of *yearning*." I had to be careful not to let the memory of my own blue balls turn into sour grapes.

When Holly visited me for the Thanksgiving holidays that year, I teased her, "Did you bring your diaphragm?"

"Oh, Daddy," she responded, "even if I fall in love with someone, it doesn't mean we have to go to bed right away."

She had found her own place on the spectrum between abstinence and promiscuity.

LENNY BRUCE
MEETS BLOW JOB BETTY

LENNY BRUCE MEETS BLOW JOB BETTY

As a friend of Lenny Bruce, as well as the editor of his autobiography, *How to Talk Dirty and Influence People*, I would've preferred this little story to have been included in the book from Lenny's point of view, but anyway...

I remember sitting in an office with a few *Playboy* attorneys. They were anxious to avoid libel, so they kept changing the name of any person in the original manuscript who might bring suit. For example, Lenny had mentioned an individual called Blow Job Betty, and the lawyers were afraid she would sue.

"You must be kidding," I said. "Do you really believe anybody would come out and *admit* that she was known as Blow Job Betty?" The book ended with a montage of Lenny's life experiences, cultural icons, folklore and urban myths:

"My friend Paul Krassner once asked me what I've been influenced by in my work.

"I have been influenced by my father telling me that my back would become crooked because of my maniacal desire to masturbate; by reading 'Gloriosky, Zero' in *Annie Rooney*; by listening to Uncle Don and Clifford Brown; by smelling the burnt shell powder at Anzio and Salerno; torching for my ex-wife; giving money to Moondog as he played the upturned pails around the corner from Hanson's at 51st and Broadway; getting hot looking at *Popeye* and *Toots and Caspar* and *Chris Crustie* years ago; hearing stories about a pill they can put in the gas tank with water but 'the big companies' won't let it out—the same big companies that have the tire that lasts forever—and the Viper's favorite fantasy: 'Marijuana could be legal, but the big liquor companies won't let it happen; [trumpet player] Harry James has cancer on his lip; Dinah Shore has a colored baby; Irving Berlin didn't write all those songs, he's got a guy locked in the closet; colored people have a special odor.'

"It was an absurd question. I am influenced by every second of my waking hour."

The lawyers edited Harry James and Dinah Shore out of that paragraph, but for some unfathomable reason, Irving Berlin remained. There was one incident, which they decided to omit entirely from the book. Lenny had been working at Le Bistro, a night club in Atlantic City. During his performance, he asked for a cigarette from anyone in the audience. Basketball star Wilt Chamberlain happened to be there. He lit a cigarette and handed it up to the stage.

"Did you see *that*?" Lenny whispered into the microphone. "He nigger-lipped it...."

Lenny and I had an unspoken agreement that there would be

nothing in the book about his use of drugs, because it could be used against him by law enforcement. When I first met him, he would shoot up in the hotel bathroom with the door closed, but now he just sat on his bed and casually fixed up while we were talking. That's what we had been doing one time when Lenny nodded out, the needle still stuck in his arm.

Suddenly the phone rang and startled him. His arm flailed, and the hypodermic came flying across the room, hitting the wall like a dart just a few feet from the easy chair in which I sat uneasily. Lenny picked up the phone. It was Blow Job Betty, calling from the lobby. She came up on the elevator and went down on Lenny after some kissing. In front of me.

Lenny had introduced us. "This is Paul, he's interviewing me." At one point, while she was giving him head, Lenny and I made eye contact. He looked at me quizzically, and his eyes said, "I'm not usually an exhibitionist."

My eyes replied, "And I'm not usually a voyeur."

A little later, Lenny said to her, "I really wanna fuck you now."

Blow Job Betty gestured toward me and said, "In front of *him*?"

"Okay, Paul," said Lenny, "I guess the interview is over now."

In retrospect, I understand the mindset of Bill Clinton when he testified under oath that he "never had sexual relations with that woman, Ms. Lewinsky." The president had simply made the same distinction between intercourse and oral sex that Blow Job Betty had made.

Incidentally, those *Playboy* lawyers insisted on changing

Blow Job Betty's name to Go Down Gussie.

"I hope there actually *is* somebody out there named Go Down Gussie," I told them, "and I hope that *she* sues *Playboy* for invasion of privacy."

IN PRAISE OF INDECENCY

IN PRAISE OF INDECENCY

The late Harry Reasoner, who was an ABC news anchor and a *Sixty Minutes* correspondent, wrote in his 1981 memoir, *Before the Colors Fade*:

"I've only been aware of two figures in the news during my career with whom I would not have shaken hands if called to deal with them professionally. I suppose that what Thomas Jefferson called a decent respect for the opinion of mankind requires me to identify those two. They were Senator Joseph McCarthy and a man named Paul Krassner or something like that who published a magazine called *The Realist* in the 1960s. I guess everyone knows who McCarthy was. Krassner and his *Realist* were part of a '60s fad—publications attacking the values of the establishment—which produced some very good papers and some very bad ones. Krassner not only attacked establishment values; he attacked decency in general, notably with an alleged 'lost chapter' from William Manchester's book, *The Death of a President*."

I appreciated Reasoner's unintentional irony—I had started as a political satirist in college, poking fun at McCarthyism—but now I resented being linked with McCarthy. He had senatorial immunity for his libels. I risked lawsuits for what I published. What I really wanted to do was crash a party where Reasoner would be. "Excuse me, Mr. Reasoner," I would have said, "I just wanted to say how much I enjoy your work on *Sixty Minutes*." And then, as a photographer captured us shaking hands, I would add, "I'm glad to meet you. My name is Paul Krassner or something like that." Instead, in 1984, when my one-person show opened, I decided to call it *Attacking Decency in General*. It ran for six months, and I received awards from the *L.A. Weekly* and *Drama-Logue*. That was my kind of revenge.

Decency is, of course, a sublimely subjective perception. And so arbitrary. In 1964, Lenny Bruce was found guilty of an "indecent performance" at the Café Au Go Go in Greenwich Village. In 2003, New York Governor George Pataki granted Bruce a posthumous pardon—but it was in the context of justifying the invasion of Iraq. "Freedom of speech is one of the great American liberties," Pataki said, "and I hope this pardon serves as a reminder of the precious freedoms we are fighting to preserve as we continue to wage the war on terrorism." Lenny would have been outraged.

Earlier that year, when rock-star/activist Bono received an award at the Golden Globes ceremony, he said, "This is really, really fucking brilliant." The FCC ruled that he had *not* violated broadcast standards, because his use of the offending word was "unfortunate," but "isolated and nonsexual." You see, it was merely an "exclamative" adjective. The FCC did not consider Bono's utterance to be indecent because, in context, he obviously didn't use the word "fucking" to "describe sexual or excretory organs or activities."

But in 2004, during a duet with Janet Jackson, Justin Timberlake sang the lyric, "Gonna have you naked by the end of this song," and in what was defended as "a wardrobe malfunction," exposed her breast for 9/16th of a second during the halftime extravaganza at the Super Bowl. I had never seen the media make such a mountain out of an implant.

In 2007, a CBS lawyer argued unsuccessfully that the network shouldn't be fined $550,000 for Jackson's breast-baring because it was fleeting, isolated and unauthorized. Nevertheless, that Nipplegate moment had provided a perfect excuse to crack down on indecency during an election year. So the FCC *reversed* their own decision, contending that Bono's utterance of "fucking brilliant" was "indecent and profane" after all.

At the 2008 Olympics, eight-gold-medals winner Michael Phelps, referring to the race where his goggles got filled with water, described it as "a wardrobe malfunction." That same year, an appeals court ruled that the FCC "acted arbitrarily and capriciously" in the Janet Jackson case, and observed that the flashing of her breast happened too fast to be considered "so pervasive as to amount to 'shock treatment' for the audience." But in November, the FCC asked the Supreme Court to appeal that ruling.

On the radio in 2003, the word "fuck" was censored out of such songs as "Fuck It (I Don't Want You Back)," "A Toast to Men (Fuck the Men)" and "She Hates Me," with a chorus of "She fuckin' hates me." Although the lyrics were bleeped in these songs, disc jockeys were forced to be creative when it came to announcing the titles. *Battlestar Galactica* invented "frak." The FCC had declared "fuck" to be "one of the most vulgar, graphic and explicit descriptions of sexual activity in the English language," no matter the context. Conservative pundit Dennis Prager characterized the fight over "fuck" as central to civilization's "battle to preserve itself."

Then, in 2005, a ray of light. The FCC ruled that isolated use of words describing private body parts—including "ass," "penis" and "testicle"—were not indecent if aired as scripted dialogue. As a self-taught semanticist, Lenny Bruce would've been intrigued by the changing attitudes toward the use of previously taboo words. He wouldn't have been able to perform on TV his classic analysis of Las Vegas, because the heart of it was about the exploitation of "tits and ass." But at the 2006 Emmy Awards, Helen Mirren and Calista Flockhart both proudly revealed that they were "ass over tits."

"If a joke is just as funny saying 'penis' rather than 'pecker,' that's fine," said Greg Garcia about his NBC sitcom, *My Name Is Earl*, "but sometimes it's funnier to say 'pecker' and that's what you have to do because it's our job to make people laugh."

In a report on NPR about Voodoo Doughnuts, a shop in Portland, Oregon, the following was deleted for fear of complaints about indecency and bad taste: "The doughnut store is holding a 'Cockfest' contest next week. Contestants, all male, will see who can put the most doughnuts on their unit. Last year's record was five. No pre-competition training—that is, Viagra—allowed."

And fast-food chain Jack in the Box was sued by rival Carl's Jr. for implying in TV commercials that its Angus beef hamburgers are made with cow anuses.

At the request of defense lawyers, a Nebraska judge ordered a college student who was raped not to use the words "rape," "victim," "assailant" or "sexual assault" on the witness stand for fear of prejudicing the jury. Perhaps she could testify, "He stuck his thing in my thing against my will." Would George Carlin have introduced a new routine in his HBO special about "The five words you can't say in court"?

A prudish school librarian tried to have an award-winning children's book, *The Higher Power of Lucky* by Susan Patron, banned because a ten-year-old orphan, who overhears someone say that he saw a rattlesnake bite his dog on the scrotum, thinks it sounded "like something green that comes up when you have the flu and cough too much. It sounded medical and secret, but also important."

In March 2007, on International Women's Day, a public high school in Westchester, New York suspended three 16-year-old girls for saying the word "vagina" during a reading from *The Vagina Monologues*. Principal Richard Leprine said the girls were punished for disobeying orders not to say the word, which he referred to on the school's homepage as "specified material." Writer Brigitte Schoen suggested calling the play *Elastic Muscular Tube Monologues*. And an episode of *30 Rock* revolved around the use of a euphemism for "cunt." That show was titled "The C Word."

At the 2007 Emmy Awards, when Katherine Heigl heard her name announced, she mouthed the word "shit." It didn't take a professional lip-reader to ascertain that. Late-night TV show hosts and sitcom characters use this "lip flap" method to say forbidden words because they *want* to be bleeped. The live studio audience laughs when they hear the uncensored version, and the home viewers figure out what's being said as if they're doing a dirty crossword puzzle.

(I once published a cartoon in *The Realist* by an artist who knew the *New Yorker* wouldn't touch it. The guest on a TV show was saying, "Frankly, I didn't give a *damn* about it!" A family watching at home heard him say, "Frankly, I didn't give a *bleep* about it!" Thought balloons showed that the mother was thinking "Fuck?" The father was thinking "Piss?" The grandmother was thinking "Shit?" And the child was thinking "Crap?")

When Sally Field accepted the best dramatic actress award for her role in *Brothers & Sisters*, her acceptance speech concluded, "Let's face it, if the mothers ruled the world, there would be no g-[*bleeped starting at this point*]oddamned wars in the first place." Ray Romano—referring to Patricia Heaton, who had played his wife on *Everybody Loves Raymond* and now had a new sitcom partner, Kelsey Grammer on *Back to You*—said, "Frasier is fucking my wife." Bleeped, of course.

Not bleeped, but apologized for on-air: Diane Keaton on *Good Morning America*, fawning over Diane Sawyer's plump lips, said she'd love to have had lips like that, because then she wouldn't have had to "work on my fucking personality." And Jane Fonda on the *Today* show, talking about *The Vagina Monologues*, told Meredith Viera, "I was asked to do a monologue called 'Cunt.'"

The award for hardcore irreverence without resorting to

four-letter words goes to Kathy Griffin. When she received an Emmy for her reality show, *My Life on the D-List*, she declared, "A lot of people come up here and thank Jesus for this award. I want you to know that no one had less to do with this award than Jesus. [*Holding up the trophy*] This award is my god now. Suck it, Jesus!" Entirely deleted.

In 2006, Isaiah Washington, a black actor on *Grey's Anatomy*, referred to fellow cast member T. R. Knight as a "faggot." Next January, at the Golden Globe Awards, he uttered the same slur while denying that he had used it previously. Faggot has become the *second* f-word in the evolution of euphemisms. Now, regarding the euphemism for fuck, "somebody said the f-word" is morphing into "somebody dropped the f-bomb." Of course, a multi-bigoted person could easily say "no s-word, that m-f-n-f ought to try out a g-d-c," meaning "no shit, that motherfucking nigger faggot ought to try out a goddam cunt." But one thing you never hear anybody say is "the n-h-h-word." It's still okay just to say "nappy-headed ho."

During the 2007 Muscular Dystrophy telethon on Labor Day, Jerry Lewis was doing a bit about imaginary family members, and he started to say to one of the show's crew members that his son, "the illiterate faggot," but stopped before reaching the g-letters, saying "no" instead, and he apologized the next day for his "bad choice of words." He was not wearing the T-shirt that says "Marriage Is For Fags." Nor, for that matter, the T-shirt that says "Fuck Yoga." Or the one that says "Fuck Frank Gehry." Or the T-shirt with a slogan "Fuck da Eagles" that Fox apologized for showing in prime time.

Camille Paglia dissed Al Gore for his "prissy, lisping, Little

Lord Fauntleroy persona" that "borders on epicene." Ann Coulter called Gore "a total fag" and John Edwards a "faggot," explaining that the word "has nothing to do with gays—it's a schoolyard taunt, meaning 'wuss'"—which, according to the *American Heritage Dictionary*, applies to men who are "unmanly." She said that Bill Clinton's promiscuity proves his "latent homosexuality," and she wrote that the odds of Hillary Clinton "coming out of the closet" in 2008 were "about even money." Hillary denied in *The Advocate*, a gay magazine, that she was a lesbian. Oh, yes, and John Gibson called Rosie O'Donnell a "fat lesbian vampire bat bully."

At the live *Billboard Music Awards* show in 2002, Cher responded to her critics, "People have been telling me I'm on the way out every year, right? So fuck 'em. I still have a job and they don't." Next year on that same awards show, Nicole Richie recounted her *Simple Life* experience: "Have you ever tried to get cowshit out of a Prada purse? It's not so fucking simple." In both instances, the FCC ruled that Fox TV had violated their standards of decency because *any* use of the word "inherently has a sexual connotation." Each violation could result in a fine as high as $325,000.

But, in what would turn out to be a pivotal decision, the FCC in 2005 reversed an indecency ruling against CBS' *The Early Show*, determining that a *Survivor* contestant calling another player a "bullshitter" did not constitute indecency because it was used in the context of a news show.

I recalled that in 1984, when I was a guest on the *Today* show, they wouldn't reimburse my airfare or hotel bill, because "We're a news show, not an entertainment show like *Good Morning*,

America." This, from *Today,* a program which once featured Willard Scott delivering the weather in Carmen Miranda drag and justifying it as entertainment. But, had NBC paid my way, it would've been "checkbook journalism." Preceding me was a segment about private corporations running prisons. During my interview, Jane Pauley asked what kind of material I would include if I were publishing *The Realist* then (a year before I re-launched it). "Oh," I replied, "I'd probably have a satire about private corporations running prisons." I later learned that the *Today* show had paid the expenses of the guest who was a corporate executive in the prison business. The line between news and entertainment was blurring.

In September 2007, a three-judge panel in a federal appeals court ruled in favor of Fox TV's challenge against the FCC for indecent and profane language. During the live court hearing, C-Span viewers were treated to such uncensored words and phrases as "motherfucker," "eat shit" and "fuck the USA." Judge Peter Hall posed a hypothetical to FCC attorney Eric Miller: "This is being fed out by cable here, and presumably the broadcast media can pick it up. Let's say they pick up a portion of [Fox lawyer Carter Phillips'] argument, and the words 'fuck' and 'shit' are actually broadcast over six o'clock news tonight. Is that going to be the subject of FCC hand-slapping?"

Miller: "I think plainly not."

Hall: "Because?"

Miller: "For the reasons stated in this very order with respect to *The Early Show* case. The commission has emphasized that it will exercise great restraint when it comes to news programs."

Hall: "Let me expand the hypothetical, to where Fox—

wanting to air, so its viewers are reminded of exactly what's at issue here—pulls up the clips from the *Billboard Music Awards* and shows those two instances of Cher and Nicole Richie, as background or in conjunction with reporting on what's happening in this courtroom here today."

Miller: "To be indecent, the use of the language has to be patently offensive, which under the commission's analysis requires that it be presented—"

Hall: "So how is a rebroadcast of the clip in the context of news any less offensive than it is in the *Billboard Awards*?"

Miller: "Because in that context, as the commission explained in *The Early Show* order, it's not being presented to pander or titillate or for shock value. It's being presented to inform viewers what the case is about."

The court reasoned that, "In recent times, even the top leaders of our government have used variants of these expletives in a manner that no reasonable person would believe referenced 'sexual or excretory organs or activities.'" The decision cited examples that had been set by the White House. It was acceptable to broadcast George Bush, captured by a live microphone, saying to Tony Blair while chewing on a mouthful of buttered roll, "See, the irony is what they [the UN] need to do is get Syria to get Hezbollah to stop doing this shit and it's over."

Similarly, it was acceptable to broadcast Dick Cheney, also caught by a live mike on the Senate floor, saying, in response to Patrick Leahy—who complained about Halliburton profiteering on the Iraq war without competitive bidding for contracts, and about Bush's judicial nominees—"Go fuck yourself." This was on the same day that the senate passed legislation, 99-1, described as "the Defense of Decency Act." The *Washington Times* reported that Cheney "responded with a barnyard epithet, urging Mr. Leahy to perform an anatomical sexual impossibility."

Nevertheless, the Bush administration appealed the Fox vs. FCC decision on "fleeting expletives," and the case was argued before the Supreme Court in November 2008. Justice John Paul Stevens wondered aloud if the word "dung" would be considered indecent. Solicitor General Gregory Garre warned that loosening indecency standards could lead to "Big Bird dropping the F-bomb on *Sesame Street*."

An appeals court has reversed the FCC's reversal in the Bono case, and suddenly he is, once again, *not* guilty of indecency. But, by June 2009, when the Supreme Court is scheduled to announce its ruling in the Cher/Richie case, the reversal of Bono's reversal could be reversed. Until then, though, it would be retroactively acceptable to broadcast Bono saying, "This is really, really fucking brilliant." Otherwise, Governor Pataki would surely have revoked his posthumous pardon of Lenny Bruce.

MASTURBATION HELPER

MASTURBATION HELPER

Pornography is a $57 billion industry—$20 billion in the United States alone, with an estimated two hundred porn flicks produced every year—devoted essentially to providing imagery for men to masturbate by. However, in Indonesia, according to an Internet factoid, the punishment for masturbation is decapitation. I don't know if that's true or not. I checked out Snopes. com, and they have nothing to say about it.

But chopping somebody's head off as punishment for playing with himself doesn't exactly fit the crime. Maybe chopping off his hand would serve justice better. Decapitation seems to be a more appropriate sentence for oral sex; at least it's closer to the scene of the crime. Meanwhile, in civilized nations, online porn has enabled countless millions of horny men to ejaculate on their keyboards. No wonder the terrorists hate us. They think our computers are *too* personal.

Islamic Voice describes masturbation as an "abominable and wicked act" that's forbidden in Islam. The Grand Mufti of Saudi Arabia stated that masturbation causes disruption of the digestive system, inflammation of the testicles, damage to the spine—"the place from which sperm originates"—plus "trembling and instability in some parts of the body like the feet," not to mention weakening of the "cerebral glands," leading to decreased intellect, even "mental disorders and insanity."

The fundamentalist Christian New Life Ministries—afraid that our sexually frustrated troops in Iraq will turn to pornography and masturbation—is making available special kits to preserve their sexual purity. Each kit comes with a workbook, a Bible study guide and a daily devotional. "You are sexually pure," GIs are told, "when no sexual gratification comes from anyone or anything but your wife."

Of course, that principle would apply to citizens too. Consider the case of Ronald Castle, Sr., a supervisor with the Department of Social Services in upstate New York. He was charged with harassment, criminal nuisance and public lewdness for masturbating into the coffee cups of fellow employees. It gives new meaning to an old romantic song, "You're the Cream in My Coffee." Plus, Ronald Castle, Jr. is blessed with a renewed sense of gratitude that he's alive today, instead of having been burned to death at the moment of his father's ejaculation and swallowed by some unknowing caffeine addict.

Rather than going to prison, Castle, Sr. should be sentenced to a kind of community service, where he can actually masturbate for altruistic reasons. Several years ago, Good Vibrations, a shop in San Francisco specializing in sex toys, erotic books and adult videos, declared the month of May to be National Masturbation Month, and a tradition was born. Since then, those in the know have been encouraged to obtain pledges from stores and individuals who sponsor their masturbatory events in cities across the country. The funds raised are donated to various sex-positive causes.

Good Vibrations' online customers were reminded: "Make sure you're well-rested, with ready hands and plenty of batteries and lube—it's Masturbate-a-thon weekend! You still have time to sign up your friends and family to help you raise money for every minute you spend masturbating this weekend. Spread the message of healthy self-love and collect funds for some excellent charities, all with a big ol' smile on your face. Download the pledge from our website. Wank on!"

Gonzo sex writer and educator Theresa Reed, known as Darklady, organized and promoted the first Masturbate-a-thon in Portland, Oregon. Her invitation stated, "Our special location will be revealed when you join the elite Benevolent Society of Masturbators. Come dressed erotically and patriotically." The party had a patriotic theme: "Masturbate Your Way to Freedom." Artist Steve Hess contributed the logo, an American eagle clutching a vibrator and a tube of lube.

The event—benefiting the National Coalition for Sexual Freedom, the Center for Sex and Culture, and Planned Parenthood—featured free food and drinks, condoms and lubrication, DJs and live bands, strippers and porn stars, door prizes and streaming video on the Internet. The ThrillHammer Orgazmatron machine proved to be a most popular competition. The woman who rode it the longest became the winner. She was crowned Miss Masturbate-a-Thon and presented with a beautiful tiara, not to mention the afterglow of multiple orgasms galore.

"Originally," Darklady told me, "I planned on hosting this party at my home, as I've had many large sex parties there. However, when I began talking to the ThrillHammer people, we decided something bigger would be in order. Being online fanatics, we definitely wanted to go beyond the more grassroots, humble masturbate-at-home events being held elsewhere. We held the party at the wonderfully pro-sex space at Ascension Dungeon and had some of the most agreeable and competent security folks I've had the privilege to work with. I was very impressed by the enthusiastic turn-out and the innovating things people did. One man brought a pyramid-like sex swing. Local cable host Harry Lime came along with his camera crew to videotape the ThrillHammer fun, and people flocked to both the camera-friendly and camera-free rooms. We had no unpleasant incidents and everyone seemed to have a great time."

There was a silent auction of goods donated by local businesses and national sex celebrities. Literature was available so that guests could learn more about the charitable groups they were helping to support. Promotional material from sponsoring companies was prominently displayed. The doors to the Masturbate-a-thon opened at 6 p.m., and the party ended at 2 a.m. Guests had to sign a liability waiver "in case you slip in your own spunk."

The main room was masturbation-free. Beyond that was a large, open space with the Orgazmatron. "ThrillHammer excitement will be broadcast live on the Internet," Darklady announced, "but the shy and saucy can protect their identity and still get a good internal massage by wearing one of the lovely masks generously donated by Bad Attitude. A modesty screen will also shield the especially shy from view. Please limit yourself to masturbation as this is, after all, a celebration of self-love."

Meanwhile, the practice of masturbation continues on and on, a 24/7 eclectic juggernaut. Following are a few examples of diversity in action.

During the trial of fertilizer salesman Scott Peterson, prosecutor Rick Distasto presented evidence that, three weeks after Peterson's wife Laci disappeared, he added a couple of hard-core porn channels to the programming on his satellite dish. Defense attorney Mark Geragos called this "as great a form of character assassination as I don't know what," although his client was on trial for the murder of his wife and their unborn child.

Peterson had added the *Playboy* channel two weeks after Laci's disappearance. Geragos argued, "There is nothing different in the Playboy channel that isn't on HBO at night"— the couple already had HBO—but Distasto pointed out that, one week later, Peterson "canceled the Playboy channel and ordered two hardcore pornography channels." Geragos asserted that, without being able to show that Laci didn't want porn in their home, the fact that her husband ordered it after she disappeared is irrelevant. "It's meant to inflame the jury," he said.

But at least Peterson jerked off in the privacy of his own living room. In Creek County, Oklahoma, 57-year-old Judge Donald Thompson was accused of frequently masturbating under his robes while his court was in session, using a special device for enhancing erections. At his trial, several witnesses—including jurors in his court and police officers who testified in trials—said that they heard the "swooshing" sound of a penis pump during trials and had seen the judge slumped in his chair, with his elbows on his knees, working the device.

Lisa Foster, who was his court reporter for fifteen years, testified: "I remember once he was using the pump during a rape trial. Another time it was during a murder trial. A baby that had been beaten to death. The baby's grandfather was teary-eyed describing the last time he had seen the baby, and the judge was up there pumping. It was sickening." In 2006, Thompson, who had been a judge for twenty-two years, was found guilty of indecent exposure and sentenced to four years in prison.

"But even the president of the United States," Bob Dylan sang, "sometimes must have to stand naked." Dylan didn't mention anything about jerking off, but, according to Monica Lewinsky in the *Starr Report*, after she performed incomplete fellatio on Bill Clinton, he would masturbate into the sink or ejaculate onto her blue dress. Clinton had previously fired Surgeon General Joycelin Elders for suggesting that we give our children sex education, which would include some information about masturbation.

Several years ago, I was at the home of a friend when someone visited him in order to borrow some pornography. It was Francis Crick, who in 1962 won the Nobel Prize in medicine for his and two others' seminal (yes, seminal) discovery of the double-helix structure of DNA. In a bestselling 1968 book, *The Double Helix*, James Watson wrote that Crick was so elated on the day of that discovery that he announced to the patrons of a local pub that the pair had just discovered "the secret of life."

Their discovery in 1953 helped launch the modern field of molecular genetics, with far-reaching implications for understanding our biology, as well as spin-offs ranging from genetic engineering to DNA fingerprinting, plus DNA imprinting found in blood, saliva and hair follicles. Certainly, to reveal that Crick liked to play with himself is not, in the words of Geragos, "as great a form of character assassination as I don't know what."

I've waited until after Crick's death to write about this, but the seemingly incongruous image of a Nobel Prize winner masturbating to porn in no way diminishes his accomplishments. There is not the slightest bit of inconsistency between his jerking off and being described by Caltech professor Christof Koch, his collaborator for many years, in these words: "He was the living incarnation of what it is to be a scholar: brilliant, rational, dispassionate and always willing to revise his own opinions and views in light of the actions of a universe that never ceased to astonish him. He was editing a manuscript on his deathbed, a scientist until the bitter end."

The *Los Angeles Times* obituary stated: "An inveterate collaborator and gatherer of thinkers about him, Crick mused over the years on questions as varied as why people dream, where life came from and whether much of the DNA in our cells was parasitic junk." Ironically, in recent years, DNA has become a euphemistic synonym for semen. So there you have it. A fertilizer salesman, a judge, a president and a Nobel laureate. Together, they represent a monument to masturbation as the Great American Equalizer.

THE MAN BEHIND
THE ARISTOCRATS

THE MAN BEHIND THE ARISTOCRATS

When I was a kid, I bought a book titled *2500 Jokes For All Occasions*. I would read each one and try to understand why it was funny. And after a while, they weren't funny; I was just analyzing them. Later on, I would read an article in the *National Enquirer*, "How To Tell a Joke," from which I learned an important piece of advice: "Always save the punch line for last."

Spoiler alert: There's a classic joke that involves a theatrical family performing all kinds of kinky sex acts—incest, scatology, bestiality—and the punch line is simply the name of their act: "The Aristocrats." The more vulgar the body of the joke, the more ironic the punch line becomes.

What I like about that joke is how the telling of it becomes like a Buddhist parable where the journey itself supercedes the destination, so that even if you already know the punch line, it can nevertheless enhance the path that will take you there. And, of course, there are variations. I even made up a clean version: This group, a family of seven, go to a theatrical agent.

"What do you do?" he asks.

"We all get together in a line, play the saxophone, wear tuxedos, our shoes are always shined, we put the sax down and do Dixieland clarinet, then we have bongo drums, with one hand we play bongos and the other hand we do double-jointed things with our fingers. For a finale we sing 'May God Continue to Bless America.'"

"And what do you call yourselves?"

"The Pukes."

Paul Provenza told me this version:

"What do you do?"

"I shit on liberals onstage."

"What do you call yourself?"

"Ann Coulter."

Provenza is an edgy stand-up comic and serious actor (he portrayed Abbie Hoffman in a stage version of the Chicago Conspiracy Trial). He is the co-producer (with Penn Jillette, the bigger and unsilent half of iconoclastic magicians Penn & Teller) and director of *The Aristocrats*, a documentary which consists of that joke being told and commented on by a hundred comedians, all performing their own, unequivocally filthy, improvised renderings.

It was the hottest ticket at the Sundance Film Festival in 2005. Originally, the plan was to play only in New York, but ultimately the movie opened around the country. Provenza interviewed me for it at a genuinely funky hotel called The Cadillac, which reveals the larger significance of the joke, the human desire to embellish reality for the sake of image. I in turn interviewed Provenza on opening night of *The Aristocrats.*

Q. What question would you like to be asked that no journalist or reporter or interviewer has asked you yet?

A. "How big is your cock?"

Q. Virtually all the people who have interviewed you can't use the language of the film that they're interviewing you about. What temptations have you had?

A. Well, you know, the funny thing is that both Penn and I will actually say that stuff anyway. And it's really funny, because they don't get mad at us, because in this context we're clearly not trying to annoy anybody. It's just kind of the nature of Hollywood.

Q. And you give the professional bleepers more jobs.

A. There's this comedian in the U. K., he did the funniest thing. He was talking about doing stand-up in America on TV. He said, "It's weird, what's that about? The next time I went back, I cursed in all the appropriate places, and they bleeped me out, but the joke was on them because I said 'cunt' in Morse Code."

Q. All those 95-year-old veterans are gonna appreciate that.

A. The best interview that we had, I think, was with [film critic]

Elvis Mitchell. And it was because not once did he mention or ask anything about obscenity. He just went right past that, and that was so refreshing. I said to him afterward, "You know, I just gotta tell you, you're the first one who's never talked about the obscenity in any way, shape or form. Why?" And he said, "Why would I waste time talking about that? I thought it was really great."

And that's one of the things a lot of people don't get—which is in some ways good and some ways bad. In some ways it's good because a lot of people are funny, and this could be kind of a breath of fresh air, thumbing your nose at the PC doctrine, the FCC and all that sort of stuff, and they're getting behind the fact that somebody's out there not playing by the rules. And you know what, no one's getting hurt.

Q. And you have that warning tagline—"No Nudity. No Violence. Unspeakable Obscenity"—in the ads. So nobody can say, "I didn't know."

A. Exactly. Although, there was one story we heard about a family that went with their kids to see a sneak preview in Florida somewhere, and they apparently thought they were gonna see the Aristo*cats*. So here's the best part. It was a half an hour before they left. They had faith in the dancing and singing cats.

Q. Maybe they thought it would be part of the act.

A. We don't want that to happen. We don't want people blind-sided. We're telling everybody, "Hey, the language can get a little rough there, come on in with us if you want." So we figure, let's be right up front about it, and some people are under the impression that that's a sort of marketing thing, that we're saying, "Hey, it's filthy, come here and see our filthy movie." That's not really our motivation. That tagline was actually Penn's idea.

He said, "I would really like this said on everything, because it says everything you need to know, and it's not that bludgeon over the head of 'Hey, come see our dirty movie.'" To me and Penn, there's so much more going on than the dirty joke. In fact, we didn't even choose this joke because it was dirty—that was secondary—we chose it because of the structure and the history of it and the fact that if you're gonna say to somebody, "We'll do this joke," imagine that, so many people know it right away, but the fact that it's dirty really had nothing to do with it.

Q. And there aren't that many jokes that allow that level of improvisation.

A. The fact that it was a dirty joke would raise other issues, and it would be interesting and would create an interesting dynamic between the movie and the audience, and also in the audience amongst themselves. But the other thing that was really cool about being a filthy joke was that people really had to let their guards down, that you can't go to these places and still be concerned about your image. And so in an effort to really get behind the scenes and really get free and loose, this joke kind of makes it impossible not to be.

Q. You could always supply masks at the box office.

A. Or those headsets that bleep it out for you. You know that new company called Clean-Film? I can't wait for them to get their hands on this one. They'd be selling like little tiny pieces of tape, "Here you go."

Q. Just the title and that's it. I'm waiting for the Pope's review: "Even worse than Harry Potter."

A. We've already made it onto a few Christian Enemies websites.

Q. That's great, because it just calls attention to rebel Christians who'd want to see it. It can't hurt, it can only help.

A. That's right. A lot of people sitting there taking notes. Reporters always ask me how it's gonna play in the red states. Well, first of all, everybody tells dirty jokes—there's nothing political about that, really—I mean, doctors, lawyers, artists, professors, astrophysicists, truck drivers, NASCAR drivers, firemen, everybody tells dirty jokes, so there really is no division, but the thing that's really frustrating is that I don't believe that there's red states and blue states.

What we have is fifty purple states. It's only a couple of thousand people in every state that makes it red or blue, and in a country of 300-million, each of those is statistically insignificant. So what we really have is fifty purple states. There's no culture war. There's just as many people in Tennessee that are on one side of this equation as there are on the other side of the equation. And this notion that these are red states basically keeps putting forward the propaganda that there's some sort of mandate. This is a crock of shit.

It's the same issue I have with the Christian Fundamentalists. It's the press, really, that's responsible for artists, distributors, networks, film studios, vendors, producers censoring themselves, because they are all under the impression that "Oh, you can't put this out there." "Oh, you can't do that." You know what? It's a crock of shit, because Eminem's still selling megaplatinum, porn is still a jillion-dollar industry, and this nonsense is just being propagated as a reality, and it's not at all.

The proof in that is very simple, which is that when you check into a hotel room, it's still $9.95 to see a titty movie, but they give you the Bible for free, because that's what people think of, they'll pay for the titties and they don't wanna pay for the Bible.

Q. That sums it up.

A. In America it works on supply and demand, that's all you need to know. The profit share. The whole Janet Jackson tit thing, we already know that two hundred people wrote thousands of letters. Meanwhile, the rest of the country was Tivoing back and forth like crazy. You know, put titties on TV and then see how many complain as opposed to how many get upset when you try to take those things away again.

Q. I once asked Ann Coulter what labels she would substitute for conservative and liberal. She answered, "Americans and cowards."

A. By the way, I wrestled her to the ground in the Green Room of *Politically Incorrect*.

Q. *You mean literally?*

A. Literally. We had a wrestling match on the ground.

Q. *Who proposed it?*

A. It just kinda happened. I looked at her, and I said, "You said the stupidest thing I have ever heard in my life," and then she asked me for a cigarette and I gave it to her, and then she said something else stupid, and I took the cigarette back and I said, "I'm not giving you anything any more, you're too stupid," and then we went for it. Hilarious. She had actually said on camera that China, all of these Asian cultures, never gave the world anything of any value until it got Christianity. And I said that is the stupidest thing I've ever heard any human being say.

Q. *And then what'd she say?*

A. "It's true." She fell to her knees, her skirt was up to her ass. That's why Bush and his fundamentalist cronies are really so dangerous, because they're really not trying to pull the wool over anybody's eyes. They really, genuinely believe this shit, and that's what's really scary. That's worse. Penn believes that she's crafting a character. He believes that she doesn't believe any of it.

Q. How many hours did you shoot for The Aristocrats?

A. We shot 140 hours, and had to edit it down to ninety minutes.

Q. Who would you like to have included that you didn't?

A. Buddy Hackett. Rodney Dangerfield. Johnny Carson.

Q. Okay, last question: How big is your cock?

A. Stand back!

SHOWING PINK

SHOWING PINK

As *Penthouse* magazine was on its way to bankruptcy, publisher Bob Guccione said, "The future has definitely migrated to electronic media." And *Hustler* publisher Larry Flynt—who eagerly joined that migration—has complained, "If you ever cruise the Net and see everything that's available, it's glutted with sleaze. It's a nightmare out there. This has to be affecting the revenues of people like myself."

But both have played pivotal roles in the evolution of popular pornography. Men's magazines had started out showing breasts but not nipples, buttocks but not anuses—and never, *never* a vagina. Nor did pubic hair used to be all over the place, only to eventually get bikini-waxed out of existence except for certain niche sites. Even nudist magazines had once air-brushed men and women into department-store mannequins without genitalia playing volleyball.

The great pubic breakthrough occurred in *Penthouse* in 1971. A triangular patch of dark curly hair eventually opened Pandora's Box wider and wider until *Hustler* began "showing pink" in 1974. Even Flynt's own wife Althea showed pink. One issue featured a Scratch-'n'-Sniff centerspread. When you scratched the spread-eagled model in her designated area, a scent of lilac bath oil emanated from her vulva.

In November 1977, Larry Flynt was flying with Ruth Carter Stapleton, the evangelist sister of President Jimmy Carter, in Flynt's pink-painted private jet, which, when it belonged to Elvis Presley, had been painted red, white and blue. Up in the air, Flynt had a vision of Jesus Christ. Flynt's entire body was tingling, and he fell to his knees, clasping his hands in prayer. Thus was he converted to born-again Christianity.

The next month, at *Hustler*'s Christmas party, Flynt announced that I was going to be the new publisher. This was the first that *I* heard the news. Before, I had been wondering how the magazine would change, and now it turned out that I was the answer to my own question. For Flynt to bring *me* in as redeeming social value was an offer too absurd to refuse.

Now that Flynt has evolved from a con artist into an authentic First Amendment hero—in July 2000, he spoke at the Commonwealth Club in San Francisco—I recall what a pariah he was in 1977. In Los Angeles, at the building in Century City, which housed his office, *Hustler* was not allowed to be listed in the lobby.

At the time, I was writing a syndicated column for alternative weeklies. Specifically, I was working on my "Predictions for 1978," leading off with this: "Since Larry Flynt has been converted to born-again Christianity, the new *Hustler* will feature a special Scratch-'n'-Sniff Virgin Mary."

"Hey, that's a great idea," said Flynt on New Year's Day at Nassau Beach in the Bahamas. "We'll have a portrait of the Virgin Mary, and when you scratch her crotch, it'll smell like tomato juice."

He was rubbing suntan lotion on my back.

"I'll bet Hugh Hefner never did this for you," he said.

Flynt wanted to know who would be an appropriate person to write an article for *Hustler* that would expose the Pope as gay. I suggested Gore Vidal, who had already stated in an interview that Cardinal Spellman was gay. So much for our first editorial conference.

There was an unwritten agreement among men's magazines that human female nipples would not be clearly visible on a cover. I was also learning to accept certain arbitrary rules then governing the inside pages. An erect penis must not be shown. Semen must not be shown. Penetration must not be shown. Oral-genital contact must not be shown.

A few months later in Georgia, Flynt was shot during a lunch break in his obscenity trial. I flew to Atlanta and went directly to the hospital. Althea brought me to Larry's room. It was extremely unsettling to see such a powerful personality so helpless, kept alive by medical technology, with one tube feeding him and another breathing for him. He appeared bug-eyed with painkiller. Althea lifted the sheet and showed me his gaping wounds, a truly awesome sight.

"Oh, God, Althea," I said, "he's showing pink."

"I'm arranging for a photographer to come in here," she said.

"We're gonna publish Larry's wounds in *Hustler*. I want people to see what they did to him."

I sat down in a chair by Larry's bed. I didn't know what to say, We simply clasped hands for a while. Finally I broke the silence. "Larry, tomorrow is Good Friday," I said. "So, uh, you don't have to go to work."

I glanced toward Althea to reassure myself that I hadn't indulged in irreverence that was *too* inappropriate, but she said, "Oh, Paul, *look*," gesturing toward Larry—"he wants to show you something." Above the oxygen mask, Larry was blinking his eyes over and over again in rapid succession.

"He's *laughing*," Althea explained.

It was a moment of unspeakable intimacy.

Althea had transformed the Coca-Cola Suite of Emory University Hospital into her office, where she was studying the slides of a "Jesus and the Adulteress" photo spread, including a semi-life-sized poster in the form of a centerfold pull-out. There was a generic barbershop-calendar Jesus, looking reverently toward the sky as he stands above the prone Mary Magdalene—almost naked, her head bleeding from the stones that have been cast upon her—and, just as the Bible says, he is covering her, *but not quite*, and she is, inadvertently, still showing pink. Sweet, shocking, vulnerable pink. This was a startling visual image, unintentionally satirizing the change from the old *Hustler* to the new *Hustler*. The marketing people were aghast at the possibility that wholesalers, especially in the Bible Belt, would refuse to distribute the magazine with such a blatantly blasphemous feature.

Faced with a crucial decision, Althea made her choice on

the basis of pure whimsicality. She noticed a pair of pigeons on the window ledge. One was waddling toward the other. "All right," she said, "if that dove walks over and pecks the *other* dove, then we *will* publish this." The pigeon continued strutting along the window ledge, but stopped short and didn't peck the other pigeon, so publication of "Jesus and the Adulteress" was postponed indefinitely. And the poster would instead remain on my wall as a memento of my six-month stint at *Hustler*. Maybe I should try to auction it off on eBay.

As for Larry Flynt's born-again conversion, he now attributes it to "a chemical imbalance" in his brain.

PEE-WEE HERMAN
MEETS PETE TOWNSHEND

PEE-WEE HERMAN MEETS PETE TOWNSHEND

Name two famous people who were both born on August 27. And the answer is: Pee-wee Herman and Mother Teresa. Okay, now, what was the reference to Pee-wee Herman that was censored out of the 1991 Emmy Awards? And the answer: Comedian Gilbert Gottfried's observation that, "If masturbation is against the law, then I should be on Death Row." This was, of course, a reference to the arrest of Pee-wee for playing with his wee-wee as he watched *Nancy Nurse* in the darkened privacy of a porn movie theater.

The bust for that victimless crime took place later in the lobby. Yes, the cops caught him coming and going. Inquiring minds wanted to know, did they force him to wash his hands before they fingerprinted him? It all seemed to be straight out of an old Lenny Bruce bit, where just such a hardened criminal must ultimately be rehabilitated by going "cold jerky."

The arrest of Pee-wee Herman might not have occurred today because, although he would undoubtedly be performing that same dastardly act of masturbation, this time it would most likely happen while he was watching porn on the computer screen in his own home. That is to say the arrest would not occur if he were watching an *adult* video.

But now he has been charged with possession of *kiddie* porn. How did this come about? A teenager had registered a complaint about Pee-wee and a friend, actor Jeffrey Jones. The complaint was dismissed, but detectives had already searched both of their homes. As a result, Jones was accused of taking pornographic photos of a juvenile, which is a felony, whereas Pee-wee faced the lesser charge of possession. If convicted of the misdemeanor, he could have been sentenced to a year in prison.

Then came the legal troubles of Pete Townshend, famed British rock guitarist and co-founder of The Who, who has admitted to downloading child pornography from the Internet for the purpose of researching the autobiography that he's writing. What follows is the transcript of my imaginary conversation between Pee-wee and Pete, based on the actual facts of their respective cases.

Pete: It's so ironic. Not only am I not a pedophile, but I have been a high profile campaigner *against* child pornography on the Web. I mean, my own grandmother sexually abused me when I was six years old. I even offered to have the hard drive of my computer analyzed by police so they could ascertain for themselves that if I did anything, which is technically illegal, it was purely for research.

Pee-wee: That's your smoking gun, silly. See, I didn't download anything, because then your credit card number becomes a matter of record. Me, I'm just a collector of vintage erotica, like those classic physique magazines that were published in the 1940s. I have 100,000 items in my archives, but none of them are from the Internet. The detectives spent a whole year studying every single one of those images, and the district attorney finally said there was no case. But then—only one day before the statute of limitations would have expired—the Los Angeles city attorney issued a warrant for my arrest.

Pete: Why? What did they find?

Pee-wee: At first they were going to charge me with possessing a tape of the actor Rob Lowe doing an underage girl, but since *he* was never charged with child porn, they changed their minds about charging me with *watching* it.

Pete: And you don't have any child pornography among your collection?

Pee-wee: Oh, there are a few minutes of grainy footage of teenage boys masturbating or performing oral sex. But I wasn't even aware of that.

Pete: Well, in England, if you possess images of children engaged in sexual activity, it's against the law, and even if you view those images *accidentally*, without really possessing them, it's still illegal.

Pee-wee: It's the same thing in the United States. If someone anonymously e-mailed child porn to me, I could be arrested for possession. Even if I immediately deleted it, that would not be acceptable as a defense.

Pete: One would think that if you happen to be an anti-porn investigator, you will be considered immune to prosecution, but unfortunately, I was not working as a *government* pervert.

Pee-wee: Hey, maybe you could prove in court that you didn't *enjoy* looking at those photos. That you *hated* the images, but you felt it was a necessary evil.

Pete: Look, the bottom line is that I am simply an innocent victim of the puritanical urge to punish.

Pee-wee: I know *you* are, but what am I?

SATIRICAL PROPHECY

SATIRICAL PROPHECY

In my capacity as a stand-up comic, several years ago I did a line on stage about a Fundamentalist Christian who had tattooed on his penis, "What would Jesus do?" Recently, that metaphorical concept which I had made up in the recesses of my warped mind came literally true. A Sunday School teacher in St. Paul, Minnesota advised one of his students to write on his penis, "What would Jesus do?" I must be careful not to let this power fall into the wrong hands.

It was a case of satirical prophecy.

In March 1991, I published in *The Realist* a satirical article by Lenny Lipton, titled "Computerized Kiddie Porn." Lipton described his meeting with a character he called Harvey, who had created—and now sells for big bucks—special computer-generated images, such as "a pretty little girl engaged in an unspeakably bestial act with an adult male who looked very much like Harvey."

Lipton wrote, "I was particularly startled by an image of a homosexual act performed on a male baby."

He asked Harvey how, in the face of a Supreme Court decision that made child pornography illegal, he nevertheless gets away with running a one-man child pornography cottage industry that brings in a six-figure income.

"It was the Supreme Court that *put* me in business," Harvey explained. "Justice Byron White, who wrote the majority opinion—it was 6-3, upholding an Ohio law—said that it's illegal to possess nude photographs of children, even if they are used privately in the home. A ban on private possession is justified, according to White, because owning such photos helps perpetuate commercial demand and thus the exploitation of helpless children. If you accept the Court's logic, then the government could intrude into the home any time a seemingly private activity is thought to perpetuate a commercial market for actions that might exploit others. This is a whole new theory of censorship, and therein lies my golden opportunity.

"You see," he continued, "no one is being exploited by my creations. These dirty pictures come out of my mind via a computer. No child is exploited. These images are perfectly legal, if I am to believe the Court is being up front with regard to the basis for its decision. As far as I am able to tell, you have nothing to worry about if you take one of my loathsome pictures home and hang it on your wall."

Back in real life, in April 2002, the Supreme Court struck down part of the federal child pornography law that makes it a crime to own or sell images of computer-created children engaged in sex. Since no actual children were portrayed in the photos and films at issue, Justice Anthony Kennedy said that the government could not make it a crime to show sexual images that only "appear to be" children.

The ruling reversed a section of the Child Pornography Act of 1996—backed by then-Senator John Ashcroft—which broadened the definition of child pornography to include any "visual depiction that is, or appears to be, a minor engaging in sexually explicit conduct," specifically mentioning a "computer-generated image or picture."

The Court's decision served to provide immunity from the law for a whole new generation of virtual child pornographers who rely entirely on computer-generated images. As long as no real children were portrayed, or morphed into a sex scene, then the photographer or filmmaker could not be prosecuted.

How had this all come about?

In 1992, a man in Texas downloaded digital files from a bulletin board system in Denmark. He was indicted for "receiving child pornography." His attorney argued that the government could not prove that the images had been made using actual children. He put on the witness stand a graphic artist, who showed how even someone with only basic computer knowledge could use a software program such as Photoshop to alter a photograph. Nonetheless, the defendant was found guilty.

Eventually, the Free Speech Coalition, a California trade association for the adult entertainment industry, went to federal court in San Francisco to challenge the law on the grounds that real children were not being exploited. That claim was rejected, but a 2-1 vote by the 9th Circuit Court of Appeals agreed that it should not be illegal to show "images of fictitious children engaged in imaginary sex acts," and the Supreme Court upheld that ruling.

Eleven years earlier, Lenny Lipton had written about his imaginary acquaintance: "Harvey lifted a print off the pile, placed it in a large manila envelope and handed it to me. I put the envelope in my briefcase and after some pleasantries I bid him *adieu*. On my drive home I thought about Harvey, the Supreme Court and the world I lived in. As I drove toward the Golden Gate Bridge, computer-generated child pornography on the seat beside me, I felt blessed to be living in a world where technology could put an end to the exploitation of children."

It was another case of satirical prophecy.

However, in February 2003, with the backing of the Bush administration, the Senate unanimously approved a revised version of the law, which would create a new definition of a minor identifiable in pornographic images as one "virtually indistinguishable" from an actual child. Moreover, defendants in criminal pornography cases would be required to provide evidence that they did not use real children to produce the images.

I guess the time has come for somebody to write a satire about the new judicial process, where an accused person is considered guilty until proven innocent. Oops, too late, that's already come true.

THE MARRIAGE OF
HIP-HOP AND PORNOGRAPHY

THE MARRIAGE OF HIP-HOP AND PORNOGRAPHY

Entertainment reporter Geoff Boucher wrote in the *Los Angeles Times*: "You might be able to imagine Garth Brooks without his cowboy hat or Britney Spears without the bare midriff... but Snoop Dogg without a joint in his hand? It may be a pipe dream, but the chronic king of hip-hop has announced that he is abstaining from marijuana as well as alcohol.

"This is shocking news considering that Snoop was named the 2002 Stoner of the Year by *High Times* magazine and has made a habit of openly toking before, during and after his concerts and interviews. He has been, arguably, the most public pothead performer since Bob Marley."

The rapper explained in an interview on BET: "I'm 30 years old now. Three kids. A wife. A mom. Brothers. Artists. Family. Friends. They all need me. They depend on me. I've been leading [homeboys] off the cliff for five, six years. So now I'm going slow."

However, then-*High Times* entertainment editor Steve Bloom considered the possibility that Snoop's surprise declaration was not necessarily a true change of heart, since he had been fined and placed on probation for a pot offense in Ohio the previous year.

"He was the biggest, baddest pot smoker out there," says Bloom (now editor of the online website *Celeb Stoner*), "and maybe he's just stepping back because it got too hot. Maybe he really has decided he wants to take a break or not smoke any more. But all this could be a smokescreen."

Sort of like when Timothy Leary and Ken Kesey, both of whom, after they were busted for dope, advised young people to stop taking LSD (*wink, wink*).

Indeed, Rollingstone.com has reported: "In a closed-door session at the Department of Justice, Snoop Dogg engaged the attorney general in a spirited debate about medical marijuana. 'The Doggfather and I have our differences,' an unusually expansive [Attorney General] John Ashcroft told reporters afterward, 'but we are both committed to relieving chronic pain.' 'Or at a mutherfuckin' minimum,' rejoined Dogg, 'relievin' with the Chronic.'"

In any case, on the Internet, Snoop's fans reacted to his announcement with both dismay and skepticism. The news also inspired commentary in Aaron McGruder's controversial comic strip, *The Boondocks*. Huey Freeman, the radical African-American kid, says, referring to Snoop's announcement, "It's the potential impact on the global economy that I'm worried about," and his little neighbor Jazmine responds, "Think he'll do a benefit song for his dealer?"

Dogg seems to have a double standard, though, when it comes to victimless "crimes." Whereas his flamboyant image once graced a cover of *High Times*, he now appears instead, seated on a throne, in full pimp regalia, on the cover of the September 2002 issue of *Adult Video News*. Their accompanying article states:

"While Snoop Dogg wasn't the first rapper to make porn—DJ Yella of N.W.A. has been producing it since the mid-1990s—*Doggystyle*, more than any other porn/hip-hop synthesis, awakened the adult industry to the immense commercial possibilities of the genre. The tape, Snoop's first collaboration with *Hustler Video*, in which he introduces the sex scenes but doesn't have sex on camera, has sold more than 150,000 units world-wide, garnering *AVN*'s Top Selling Tape of 2001 Award... Largely due to the success of *Doggystyle*, more and more rappers are appearing in porn videos with no fear of alienating fans."

Snoop believes that the hip-hop/porn connection benefits both industries. "The adult video world is so much what rap music is all about," he says in *Adult Video News*, "about expressing ourselves and having fun, and a lot of times radio and TV don't understand that so they censor us. So I feel like we're doing each other justice by being hand in hand and working with each other. I mean, a lot of people be in the closet about it, but they all listen to rap music or watch adult videos one way or another.

"I always wanted to do it because I felt like I had a lot of records that would never get no airplay or never get no visuals, and I just wanted to make some type of video where I could do these songs and have naked ladies in them and doing that type of shit. And then when I figured out that I could make a whole movie, I got with the right director and then put my ideas down and made it happen."

Speaking of his follow-up to *Doggystyle*, titled *HUSTLAZ, Diary of a Pimp*, he expounds, "It's just basically the day in the life of a pimp, everything he's got going on with all the ladies in different rooms in the house and different situations that occur. And videos. So it's just like a live, put-together movie. It's a diary. It's like a documentary in movie fashion. We made three new records ['Break These Hoes for Snoop,' 'Doin' It Too' and 'Pussy Like This'] that were just specifically for this, where we could make records that was hot and we knew they were X-rated and they would fit the movie, fit the theme. This shit is hot, when it's all side by side, the videos and the acting and the music all comes together."

Apparently, Snoop Dogg's family—those three kids, his wife and his mother—are all completely supportive of his current activity. And so he maintains a hard-on all the way to the bank. Snoop's new public agenda can be summed up in four little words: "Porn, *si*. Pot, *no*."

PORN AND
THE MANSON MURDERS

PORN AND THE MANSON MURDERS

The recent TV movie, *Helter Skelter*, perpetuated the myth of Charles Manson. In 1969, when the news broke about the massacre of pregnant actress Sharon Tate and her house guests, there was a sudden epidemic of paranoia in certain Hollywood circles. Actor Steve McQueen fled to England, for example, and I wondered why. After the trial of Manson and his brainwashed followers, I began my own private investigation, if only to satisfy my sense of curiosity about the case.

I corresponded with Manson, visited Charlie's Devils in prison, including Susan Atkins, and—in a classic example of participatory journalism—I took an acid trip with a few family members, including Squeaky Fromme, who is now behind bars for the attempted assassination of then-President Gerald Ford.

Ed Sanders' book, *The Family*, had mentioned that Los Angeles police had discovered porn flicks in a loft at the crime scene, the home Tate shared with her director husband, Roman Polanski (who was in London at the time of the murders). And yet, the prosecutor in Manson's trial, Vincent Bugliosi, denied in his book, *Helter Skelter*, that any porn flicks had been found. It was possible that the police had indeed uncovered them but lied to Bugliosi.

I learned why when I consulted the renowned San Francisco private investigator, Hal Lipset, whose career had been the basis for an excellent film, *The Conversation*, starring Gene Hackman. Lipset informed me that not only did Los Angeles police seize porn movies and videotapes, but also that individual officers were *selling* them. He had talked with one police source who told him exactly which porn flicks were available—a total of seven hours' worth for a quarter-million dollars.

Lipset began reciting a litany of those porn videos. The most notorious was Greg Bautzer, an attorney for financier Howard Hughes, together with Jane Wyman, the former wife of then-Governor Ronald Reagan. There was Sharon Tate with Dean Martin. There was Sharon with Steve McQueen. (That was a silent *Aha!* moment for me, since one of the victims was Jay Sebring, Hollywood hair stylist and drug dealer to the stars.) There was Sharon with two black bisexual men.

"The cops were not too happy about *that* one," Lipset recalled.

There was a video of Cass Elliot from the Mamas and the Papas in an orgy with Yul Brynner, Peter Sellers and Warren Beatty. Coincidentally, Brynner and Sellers, together with John Phillips of the Mamas and the Papas, had offered a $25,000 reward for the capture of the killers.

I always felt the executioners had a prior connection with their victims. I finally tracked down a reporter who had hung around with police and seen a porn video of Susan Atkins with one of the victims, Voytek Frykowski. When I asked Manson about that, he responded: "You are ill advised and misled. Sebring done [sic] Susan's hair and I think he sucked one or two of her dicks. I'm not sure who she was walking out from her stars and cages, that girl *loves* dick, you know what I mean, hon. Yul Brynner, Peter Sellers..."

Meanwhile, Charlie has become a cultural symbol. In surfer jargon, a "manson" means a crazy, reckless surfer. For comedians, Manson has become a generic joke reference. I asked him how he felt about that. He wrote back: "I don't know what a generic is, Joke. I think I know what that means. That means you talk bad about Reagan or Bush. I've always ran poker games and whores and crime. I'm a crook. You make the reality in court and press. I just ride and play the cards that were pushed on me to play. Mass killer, it's a job, what can I say."

But Manson has apparently been moonlighting, because his new CD, *All the Way Alive*, was recently released. He was discussing with the producer of his album the notion that people's public images can be vastly different from the way they behave in their private lives. As an example, Charlie mentioned "the sex movies Steve McQueen and Peter Sellers were doing with Sharon Tate."

RAPE AND PORN

RAPE AND PORN

The month of May is not only National Masturbation Month. It has also been designated as Teen Pregnancy Prevention Month. Isn't it encouraging when different causes can work together with such perfect symbiosis? And yet, the late, ever-provocative novelist Norman Mailer—fearless in the face of political correctness—was opposed to both birth control *and* masturbation. Here are a few excerpts from my 1962 interview with him:

"The fact of the matter," Mailer was saying, "is that the prime responsibility of a woman probably is to be on earth long enough to find the best mate possible for herself, and conceive children who will improve the species. If you get too far away from that, if people start using themselves as flesh laboratories, if they start looking for pills which prevent conception, then what they're doing, what really at bottom they're doing, is acting like the sort of people who take out a new automobile and put sand in the crank case in order to see if the sound that the motor gives off is a new sound."

"You're forcing me to the point of personalizing this," I said. "Do you use contraception? Do you put sand in your crank case?"

"I hate contraception."

"I'm not asking you what your attitude toward it is."

"It's none of your business. Let me just say I try to practice what I preach. I *try* to."

"Then you believe in unplanned parenthood?"

"There's nothing I abhor more than Planned Parenthood. Planned Parenthood is an abomination. I'd rather have those fucking Communists over here."

At one point, Mailer said that "a native village is bombed, and the bombs happen to be beautiful when they land; in fact it would be odd if all that sudden destruction did not liberate some beauty. The form a bomb takes in its explosion may be in part a picture of the potentialities it destroyed. So let us accept the idea that the bomb is beautiful. If so, any liberal who decries the act of bombing is totalitarian if he doesn't admit as well that the bombs were indeed beautiful."

"Aren't you implying that this beauty is an absolute?"

"Well, you don't know. How do you know beauty is not an absolute?"

A little later, I asked, "Is it possible that you have a totalitarian attitude toward masturbation?"

"I wouldn't say all people who masturbate are evil, probably I would even say that some of the best people in the world masturbate. But I am saying it's a miserable activity."

"Well, we're getting right back now to this notion of absolutes. You know—to somebody, masturbation can be a thing of beauty—"

"To what end? Who is going to benefit from it?"

"It's a better end than the beauty of a bombing."

"Masturbation is bombing. It's bombing oneself."

"I see nothing wrong if the only person hurt from masturbation is the one who practices it. But it can also benefit—look, Wilhelm Stekel wrote a book on auto-eroticism, and one of the points he made was that at least it saved some people who might otherwise go out and commit rape."

"It's better to commit rape than masturbate. Maybe, maybe. The whole thing becomes difficult."

"But rape involves somebody else."

"Just talking about it on the basis of violence: one is violence toward oneself; one is violence toward others. Let's follow your argument and be speculative for a moment—if everyone becomes violent toward themselves, then past a certain point the entire race commits suicide. But if everyone becomes violent toward everyone else, you would probably have one wounded hero-monster left."

"And he'd have to masturbate."

"That's true…. But—you use that to point out how tragic was my solution, which is that he wins and still has to masturbate. I reply that at least it was more valuable than masturbating in the first place. Besides, he might have no desire to masturbate. He might lie down and send his thoughts back to the root of his being."

Mailer concluded that "The ultimate direction of masturbation always has to be insanity." He didn't mention anything about going blind or becoming a hunchback or growing hair on the palm of one's hand.

But now I have a question for myself. Since I oppose government interference in the content of pornography, how do I feel about such things as virtual rape on the Internet?

Although the California Supreme Court has declared that a man may be convicted of rape if his sexual partner first consents but later changes her mind and asks him to stop, a victim of date rape is unable to take advantage of that ruling. As a preventive measure, there's a new product on the market—paper coasters which theoretically test for date-rape drugs—ringing up more than $20-million a year in revenue. These coasters have test spots, which are supposed to turn dark blue in thirty seconds if a splash of alcohol contains drugs that are often used to incapacitate victims.

When Andrew Luster, the millionaire great-grandson of cosmetics tycoon Max Factor, was on trial for date rape, his defense attorneys attempted unsuccessfully to prove that he was actually an aspiring porn producer who was merely practicing his craft when he directed films in which women were only pretending to be asleep while he had sex with them, and that Luster actually intended to sell his porn flicks on the Internet.

The lawyers were foiled in their attempt to show excerpts of Luster's home-made movies in order to counter testimony from women who would testify that they were drugged and raped at his beach house. Ironically, there are *actual* porn producers who merchandise rape videos, and they *too* claim that the women who are sexually assaulted are merely pretending to be raped. They may really be raped, who knows, but these companies are simply attempting to cover their *own* asses.

Scream and Cream includes this blatantly misspelled disclaimer on their website: "All models herein depicted were over 18 at the time of depiction and were copmensated [*sic*] for their play. We do not condoce [*sic*] nondone [*sic*] non-nocensual [*sic*] sex. This site is forced sex *fantasy* only."

Another site, *Forced Girls*, can't even spell their own name, as they promote "The #1 forsed [*sic*] site on the net." And here's their come-on: "Tired of seeing teens all over the net that look older than your mom? We are too, this is why we created this jam packed with only the youngest, barely legal girls forced to fuck and suck, prosecuted [*sic*] by their capturers and brutally punished."

The *Shocking Extreme* site states, "Warning: Exclusive Content," as though exclusivity were something kinky and forbidden. "She has no hope of escape," they boast. "These guys are pro's [*sic*]."

Uncensored Russian Rapes describes itself as a "Unique Russian rape site with fully exclusive Russian content. Different rape situations, pictures like rape with weapons, rape in the cars, gang rape, amateur rape plus hundreds of real rape movies."

There is an urban legend in Russia that having sex with a virgin will cure AIDS. This dangerous myth has resulted in an epidemic of HIV-infected males violating virgins, especially teenagers, because of their insane belief that the younger the virgin, the more potent the cure.

"Do you want to rape a virgin too?" asks the site. "Enter at your own risk."

Although I don't believe that those who download sexual-assault pornography should be arrested, I do think that those who *produce* rape porn should get busted—but only if it can be proven that the sex was non-consensual, and that ain't easy. In fact, it's virtually impossible.

In *The Village Voice*, Johnny Maldoro wrote about a video by porn director Lizzy Borden: "Part fictional snuff, over-the-top gore, and violent hard-core porn, *Forced Entry* won't be taking home any *AVN* [Adult Video News] awards, and might even force the mainstream media to momentarily focus on our country's largest entertainment industry.... To prove that her actresses knew what they were signing up for, Borden tacks a bunch of bloopers onto the end of *Forced Entry*. Veronica Caine's wig comes off! Other wacky antics on the set prove the non-exploitative and even friendly relations between cast and crew members! For instance, Taylor St. Claire is totally 'not pregnant.' Those guys weren't jumping on a *real* fetus."

In Pakistan, the main human rights group reveals that in 2002, at least 461 women were slain by family members in so-called "honor killings." In such cases, women are murdered to protect the "family honor" for "offenses" such as dating, talking to men, having sex outside marriage, cooking poorly—and being raped.

Whereas, here in the United States, there was a TV documentary about a church-sponsored "Hell House"—which was intended to scare religious teenagers out of engaging in *any* kind of sexual activity—but one girl's reaction is worth placing in a time capsule for future reference.

"The rape scene is the best," she said, "because you get to dance."

BIZARRE SEXUALLY ORIENTED SPAM SUBJECT LINES

BIZARRE SEXUALLY ORIENTED SPAM SUBJECT LINES

Every one of the spam senders in this informal survey is trying—
in the hope that you won't immediately press the delete key—to
entice you into checking out their messages and purchasing their
products. In that process, they will sometimes deliberately (but
not always deliberately) misspell words in the subject lines of
their spams in order to bypass any electronic filters you happen
to set up.

A friend writes to me, "I just upgraded to AOL 9 which has
a feature that takes out spam before it gets to you. Theoretically you submit and save a list of words you don't want in your
subject line—in my case some are Viagra, Xanax, cheerleaders
and mortgages—then voila! But, as always, the spammers are
one step ahead. Now I'm getting spam for Viagara, Xannax,
cheer leaders and mort.gages—then *voila!* I don't know why
they think I'd do business with anyone whose spelling skills

were so faulty, but I guess their target audience may not care."

And from another friend: "Has anyone had a problem with blocked e-mail? I have had fully one-third of my mail blocked by my ISP that is running Norton's 'Barracuda Spam Firewall.' *Phooey!* It blocks e-mail from friends and newsletters but lets the porn, Viagra and 'grow your penis pills' through. I am ticked! Anyone else all of a sudden not hearing from friends?"

Meanwhile, federal agents have arrested a man for repeatedly making death threats against employees of an Internet advertising firm. He faces a maximum penalty of five years in prison and a $250,000 fine if convicted. He had mistakenly believed that the company was the source of unsolicited e-mail ads he received about penis enlargement. Well, everyone has his breaking point.

Carol Liefer observed on Comedy Central that apparently there are a lot of people who want *her* to have a bigger penis. And, on the all-female morning TV talk show, *The View*, this rhetorical question was posed: "Which is worse, a tiny little penis or a lot of violence?" As if in response, a dwarf detective on a Comedy Central promo for their movie, *Knee-High P.I.*, observed, "Sometimes the best dick is a small dick," though you'll never see *that* in a subject line.

Anyway, here's a quaint selection of penis-enlarger subject lines: There's the impress-a-female approach—"Women have always said: Size Matters!"... "No girl will give U a damn if U have little penis"... "Hey My Girl Bought Me the Patch"... "She likes my new weenie"... "I am lookin for a big man like U! C*U*M* to me!"... "Wanna be big enough to shock people?"... "You will leave her speechless"... "Make her scream OHHH YEAAA!"

But men also like to impress *other* men, as in "Feal proud when your in the locker room" and "Your friends will envy you"—(guaranteed up to 4 rock hard inches).

Plus some more choices for the road: "gipzyxdtcbidvd + yeilopcecsu"... "Keep praying eyes away!"... "Monster Cocks at Discount Price"... "impede her ybpajh"... "dont worry about ur stupid little penis, ha ha"... "do u think u still can fuck like those who has macho dick?"... "Every man wishes he had a larger penis"... "Be a man and add a third leg"... "Enlarge your Manhood"... "Increase your penis size in one day"... "my hole was bored out by the reaper"... "Be happy when you make love!"... "With these pills you can shoot cum like a porn star!"... "Penus Enlarged in 2 Hours!"

The misleading subject line is a popular method of tricking you. "Tickets arrived" led to this message: "there is no other way to enlarge your penis." This vague subject line—"Hey, shit happens"—and this non sequitur subject line—"Do you like oranges?"—both led to the same message: "Use this patch and it will grow i SWEAR...."

All right, so now the good news is that every man has a larger penis. However, the bad news is that none of them can get it *up*.

"I remember a spam," writes a friend, "about free Viagra after a penis enlargement operation that would take place someplace in Nigeria just before the search for my share of several hundred million dollars that my new friend is cutting me in on. Seems his dad stashed bullion in foreign accounts to which they'd have no access until I brought several thousand dollars first. Could have gotten way rich while erect for days while I fucked myself."

Another friend quotes a spam—"Massive rock-solid Erections, new natural product bmrgwhmsmnmb"—and adds, "I like how it turns into nonsense at the end. I kind of picture like it's a mild mannered guy at the beginning who takes the 'natural' Viagra somewhere in the middle and then by the end he's like the incredible Hulk with a hard-on so powerful he can't even make coherent sounds. Also: 'From Keith Moon: Re: Generic Viagra'—At least they have a sense of humor. Maybe they'll start coming from 'Rush Limbaugh' next."

And now for your reading pleasure, here's an erection selection:

"Stick it on you then stick it to her" (Viagra-like patch)..."Beef up the size of your willy"... "Bob Dole loves Viagra, so should you!"... "terrifying terpsichorean"... "The Assay Test"... "Men let the pillz do the talking"... "Is it time to upgrade your system?"... "You will be a sex machine"—(erectile dysfunction)... "condolence maverick expedition"... "Goodbye to Soft Equipment"... "Are you hard at work?"

"You blocked my ICQ"... "ur di.cky is so smalllll"... "Enh.. anc,e_yo*ur RO...D"... "G*et a ,*B-UL^;K,Y 'PO*L;E'"... "Incr*eas^e :D"IC^-K :LENGTH' easil'y"... "B^oost y-our c'onf'ide;nc,e"... ",T:h_e na_tio*na:l i;nfrast*ru:ctu re i:s fal: li^ng"

"Stay hard for 72 hours"—*Editor's note*: Viagra ads in magazines state: "You should call a doctor immediately if you ever have an erection that lasts more than 4 hours. If not treated right away, permanent damage to your penis could occur."

This vague subject line—"Hi"—led to this message: "Sometimes people call it 'Magic Lubricant.' Sometimes 'Power Bottle.' Why? An amazing erection WITHIN SEVERAL SECONDS is guaranteed to you! Double-strengthed orgasm and full satisfaction)."

Both "Can I Make It Up to You?" and "One Last Question" are spam subject lines for this message: "Did you know you could discreetly order Viagra over the Internet? You don't have to go through all the problems of getting it in a local pharmacy store or explaining your problems to the doctor." And then there was this charming misleader: "Enlarge your Bank Account 2-3 inches in days."

Okay, so now all these horny men have gigantic penises and also the medical means to help them defy gravity and become oh so erect, but there's simply nobody around with whom to share these huge hard-ons. That's where the Internet porn industry will eagerly come to your rescue.

"Amateur Girls Never Before Seen"... "Fresh hot assets"... "Drunk party babes"... "Wow—Screwing Machines"... "Bondage at Mistress Shaved's Nasty Fetish Club"... "Pussies Getting Slammed"... "Pregnant Girls Getting Laid!"... "Look inside a pussy with our dildo-cam"... "watch this girl get her poousy lips get parted with a tongue"... "Big Clits—Monster Clits"... "enter this place and you willl see hard nipples and pink beavers"... "I have a multi-colored bush for you to see"... "The Executive's Dream"—(your secretary is a dirty little thing, and wants your Man Meat!)

Hey, *psst*, you wanna see some nice breasts? Try these for size: "All we have are Breasts!"... "Do You Like Tits"—(100,000+ pics of big titty girls)... "Big Huge Breasts"... "Melon size boobies"... "Jumbo Juggy Jugs"... "Big juicy titties"... "Petite Little Boobs... "

How about interracial? "Choked white whores used as black cum recepticals"... "White Ladies and Dark Meat Look of Pain!" Or what about international? "Nasty Asian sex"... "Viet Yummy"... "Latin girls getting fucked"... "Re: travel plans"—(We've got girls from countries all over Asia spreading their pink pussies)... "I put the stalian back in Italian...."

Do you prefer four-legged friends? "Watch me fuck a poodle"... "Oh my God, I had S-E-X With My Dog!"... "Meet Harvey the pussy eating wonder dog!"... "Teen takes a horse dong deep inside her flower"... "She takes the 20 inch horse pole"... "The real farm movie they tried to ban"—(guess Ramo's [the horse's] cock size and win a free ticket to the show)... "Dacy Does Donkeys"... "S*X WITH PETS"—(Taken to the Xtreme)... "This is sicker than Michael Jackson's daycare"—(girls with farm animals)... "Hot women do everything in my car"—(You ever wanted to see a live donkey show?) *Editor's note*: Gosh, that must be a very large car.

You dig first-timers? "Angel's First Facial"... "Erika's First five finger Experience"... "First Time Lesbians!"

Know how to make (or take) a fist? "Miss Fist-a-Lot!"... "Porn Queens Fistfucked for Real"... "Get Your Fisting Party Started!"

Got oral sex? "Cum Squad Squat!"... "Free pics of teen Sluts Sucking Almighty Cocks!"... "Teens covered in cum!"... "Young Pussy Lickers"... "Girls love to tasty cum"... "Shooting Incident"—(Max Cumshot)... "See them spurt!"—(Cumshakes, Thousands of Hot Cum Covered Girls)... "I blew my load all over her"—(Facial Fiasco)… "She swallowed it all, Cum splattered all over her face"… "Jizz drizzled all over my face help me!"… "Sarah sucking balls"… "Bite that cock!"

Or maybe anal? "Doing Her Ass"… "My Girl Likes Anal Sex"… "Nasty Girls Doing Backdoor"… "I've applied to 4 Universities, but this one has the best programs"—(We're going to send you to Anal University).

Golden shower, anyone? "She's a Pee Fanatic!"… "She peed on me!"

Age is no barrier: "Virgin Schoolgirls"… "Cranky debutantes"… "Teen sluts gone wild"… "Tight Teen Cunts"… "watch me spread this teens Pucey lips"… "Ordinary Girls with Spread Legs—naughty girls fresh out of high school"… "Cute girls in college spreading their legs"… "Aged woman spreads legs"… "Loving for grannies"… "Hot Nude Granny"—(The Premier Mature Lady Site).

Neither is gender a barrier. "Crazy Gay Action only the BIGGEST Gay Cocks Inside"… "New reality site with young boys"… "Gay closet movies"… "sex crazed lesbians"…

Nor marriage vows. "I'm ready to cheat on my husand"… "With the kids asleep, mom gets wild and kinky"… "Sit back, relax and get a blow job from a woman at EZ Cheatng tonight"… "watch these ladies get nailed while the kids are in bed"… "in here is over 5 hundred thousand pictures of hot moms naked"… "Look at a hot mom taking a shower and shaving her vagina"… "The State Survey"—(How many children do you claim? Real yummy mummys)… "Don't Be Shy" and "Please don't tell anyone"—(both lead to "a revolutionary new service connecting cheating wives with single men.")

Celebrities in homemade sex videos are of course a special treat on the World Wide Web, from Pamela Anderson to Paris Hilton. From "Paris Hilton just drinks love juice" and "Paris Hilton is on a see men diet" to "J. Lo's Nipples" and "J. Lo caught eating a booger"—whatever turns you on.

Here, have a subject-line montage: "Bob said you'd want this"... "Naked Girls Next Door"—(Enter here to fuck these hot girls)... "(no subject)"—(Do you ever find yourself thinking about what it would be like to see naked girls all day?)... "lusty transvestites take picture for you"... "Upskirt panty peaks"... "Her cherrry gets popped!"... "Watch these young teens get exploited—severely!"... "100% hot bitches"... "As vulg@r as it getz"... "The sickest place on earth"—(midgets, animals, trannies, fisting, pregnant, enemas)... "Unreal Penetrations"... "Security Guards F_ucking Hot Girls"... "Take care"—(Insane orgies)... "3 Girls gang-banged"... "These Guys Don't have a Chance!"—(Hot Young locals Seduce Unknowing Tourist!)... "Stop wasting money on women!"

These are spam subject lines that have a certain sexual aura, but lead you to non-sexual messages: "Do you know I love you"—(money lender)... "See my newest movie"—(Wholesale prescription medicines)... "As good as it gets"—(online poker)... "It is hard"—(Banned CD, Government don't want me to sell it. Your own FBI file, driving record, criminal databases)... "We Got the Spread"—(Nude, but click here to bet now! NFL odds)... "Beach Girls"—(Forget Aging and Dieting forever)... "First Time"—(for both "Wholesale prescription medications at bargain prices" and "Term-life coverage at reduced rates is now available")... "I can come" and "Corrupted existentially" both lead to weight-loss messages.

Or, a subject line can appear to be political, such as "How Saddam Survived," which turned out to be a pitch for a growth hormone releaser from the American Society For the Treatment of Aging.

And finally, here's my own personal favorite spam, which came from DarkProfits.com. The subject line reads: "Your credit card has been charged for $234.65"—which leads to the following message, headlined *Important Notice*:

"We have just charged your credit card for money laundry service in amount of $234.65 (because you are either child pornography webmaster or deal with dirty money, which require us to laundry them and then send to your checking account). If you feel this transaction was made by our mistake, please press 'No.' If you confirm this transaction, please press 'Yes' and fill in the form below. Enter your credit card number here. Enter your credit card expiration date."

In the immortal words of Bart Simpson, "I didn't think it was physically possible, but this both sucks and blows."

Postscript: Had to share this one: Spam subject line: "Ethan is the paper ready yet?" The message: "Make her scream with joy! Become the 9 incher today!" Also, 40 days before the 2004 presidential election, I spotted a new—though temporary— trend. Here are a few subject lines, courtesy of Viagra: "Kerry Isn't Feeling Well"; "George Bush Is A Liar"; and "Breaking News: Osama Bin Laden Captured."

MEET AN FBI PORN SQUAD AGENT

MEET AN FBI PORN SQUAD AGENT

In October 2006, a historic event occurred in the world of porn. Seven FBI agents sat down to engage in a dialogue with a group of "adult businesspersons," as Mark Kernes wrote in *AVN*. The purpose of this meeting at FBI headquarters was to discuss plans to implement federal regulation 2257, which requires producers to obtain two forms of government-issued identification from performers, keep them on file indefinitely, and refer to those records on the labels of all videos and DVDs. How mundane.

One of the attorneys who was present—Jeffrey Douglas, chairman of the Free Speech Coalition—says that complying with the rules has buried porn producers in paperwork. One of his clients employs a staff of eight who work full-time to maintain and organize the required records. "If you were so incredibly crazy to film a minor," he observes, "you surely would not get a copy of their junior high school ID." He points out that although the FBI said its "primary concern" is underage performers, it inspects all the records for the video features on its list, creating a report that it forwards to the Department of Justice (DOJ).

Another attorney, Paul Cambria, recalls, "They said they created a database of producers, they fed it into a computer, and the computer spit out, randomly, companies to be inspected. The FBI agents then review that company's product. They then select certain individual actors and actresses, then go to a [place of business] with the list, and look for the required records as to those people." Cambria asked the assistant director of the criminal investigation division, James "Chip" Burrus, "whether it was based on any particular content, and he said no. So I said, 'There are certain movies, for example, that are of a sort of geriatric genre; why would you waste your time?' And he said, 'No, we include those because we want to keep it all random at this point.'"

In *AVN*, Kernes wrote that "*Any* violation of the 2257 regulations may result in federal charges being brought, with penalties including fines and years in jail for each violation.... So while the FBI's function is merely to inspect the 2257 records to ascertain whether they are complete and accurate, the report the bureau files with the Justice Department could easily form the basis for decisions as to which companies the DOJ may choose to prosecute for obscenity, knowing that a bona fide 2257 violation by a company would be an incentive for that company to cop a plea."

Three months later, the *Los Angeles Times* reported that the FBI has stepped up raids on porn studios, "saying it wants to ensure that children are not being sexually exploited. About a dozen porn production facilities... have been taken by surprise in the last three months by a barrage of federal agents at their doors.... The Justice Department has prosecuted only one company to date under the new law... the founder of the *Girls Gone Wild* video empire, Joe Francis."

One of the raided companies, K-Beech, Inc.—comprised of fifteen studio lines that feature titles in a variety of niches, including straight, gay, amateur, transexual and gonzo—takes the storyline out of adult movies and heads right for the sex scenes. Early one morning, the agents demanded to see the offical IDs certifying that performers in ten sexually explicit films dating back to 1995 were not minors. They weren't.

Owner Kevin Beechum asks, "Why would I jeopardize $10-million a year to shoot an underage girl? We're not stupid."

Historian Athan Theoharis states that "The FBI has limited what they investigate since 9/11, so moving into this area does raise the question of resources. Is this at the expense of investigating the Enrons or the WorldComs that have far more effect on the lives of American citizens?" In that same vein, a letter to the *Times* asks, "If the FBI can send agents out to porn studios to check employee records, then it's now clear that all terrorists, bank robbers, kidnappers and miscellaneous fugitives have all been caught and locked up. Haven't they?" In another letter, Georgina Spelvin, who starred in the 1973 classic porn flick, *The Devil in Miss Jones*, writes, "My heart goes out to the poor FBI agents required to spend hours viewing porn, 'culling material in search of performers with a suspiciously youthful glow.' What a bum assignment."

And so the FBI has become part of the Bush administration's War on Porn. When the Bureau's Washington Field Office began recruiting for their fledgling obscenity squad, ten agents were selected. What follows is my apocryphal interview with one of them, who of course prefers to remain anonymous.

Q. Why do you think that this undertaking was described in a memo to all 56 FBI field offices as "one of the top priorities" of Attorney General Alberto Gonzales and FBI Director Robert Mueller?

A. I think they figure that pornography is an easy target. It's what Congress asked for, and funded. Nobody wants to come out *for* porn. They're all sucking up to the religious right. Plus they're control freaks themselves. And this operation misdirects attention away from the results of their own insidiousness and incompetence. To tell you the truth, the guys I had worked with, they all thought it was just a big joke.

This was in an FBI field office where there are *really* important projects—involving national security, high-technology crimes and public corruption—but I was feeling burnt out. I needed something less stressful. So I applied for the "Hard-On Hunters," which is how my old buddies refer to it. They still razz the hell out of me. One guy says, "Hey, I thought there was supposed to be a war on *terror* going on." Then another guy says, "Yeah, and I thought it was supposed to be urgent that we develop better resources for espionage." And the first guy says, "I guess we must have been wrong."

Q. So what exactly is it that you do in your new mission?

A. Well, we have to gather evidence against the manufacturers and purveyors of pornography. And it's not even the kind that exploits children—I mean, I'm totally against kiddie porn—but this is about the kind of material that's marketed to consenting adults. I never liked pornography myself—they used to show it at my college fraternity—but when I first joined the FBI, I swore to uphold the Constitution, not to trample on the Bill of Rights.

In fact, the communiqué we got from the Justice Department even admitted that federal obscenity prosecutions encounter many legal issues, including claims of 1st Amendment rights, so we applicants had to be prepared for the kind of material that tends to be most effective with local juries, because it's been shown that the best odds of conviction are in pornography cases that involve bestiality, urination, defecation, sadism and masochism. But it's a living.

Q. How have you gone about doing your job?

A. I started out with bestiality fetishes as my specialty. In the course of my research, I checked out websites with beautiful women actually having sex with all kinds of animals.

Q. So tell me, did you get aroused?

A. Actually, yes, I did, but I was aroused only by the women, not by any of the animals. Later on, though, I was investigating a whole variety of kinky sites—from female ejaculators who are squirtaholics to tobacco addicts who smoke before, during and after sex—and then I found one that was devoted entirely to women who wear eyeglasses and the men who love to come on them, that is, on the glasses, while they're being worn, and somehow that really turns me on.

I've become obsessed with it. I'm seeing a psychiatrist twice a week now. She practices hypnotic age regression, and she took me all the way back to when I was being breast-fed, and my mother wore glasses, and that became associated with sensuality. And now that I understand the cause of my fixation, I can begin to wean myself from it.

Q. *What's next for you, then?*

A. Well, I've learned that digitalized pornography on cell phones is a huge business overseas, and it's coming to America. Cingular Wireless, the country's largest cell phone service, has quietly launched filtering devices and password-enable blockers that will help thwart underage consumers from buying adult content. But what we're more concerned about is a new trend where adult film stars make groaning and moaning noises for cell phone ring tones. It feels like the whole world is getting completely out of control—*our* control.

REMEMBERING PUBIC HAIR

REMEMBERING PUBIC HAIR

Okay, call me old-fashioned, but I still like pubic hair. Internet porn sites now present several choices—completely shaved, vertical landing strips that look like exclamation points, heart shaped, the Charlie Chaplin with just a little patch above the clitoris, and a tiny triangle that serves as an arrow *pointing* to the clit—yet, for pubic follicles one has to search the Web for "hairy" sites that are considered as "specialty," "kinky" or "fetish."

Retired porn stars have commented on this phenomenon. Gina Rome, retired after six years, shaved every day. "It was part of getting ready for work." When she switched from acting to film editing, she stopped shaving and let her pubic hair grow out. "Shaving was work. I don't have to do it any more, so I don't." And Kelly Nichols says, "I was a *Penthouse* model in the early 1980s, and I posed with a full bush. No one in adult entertainment shaved back then. Now everybody does."

Although Martha Stewart is back on TV, you can be sure that she'll never give any suggestions on what to do about those big red razor bumps that result from shaving your vagina, so here's a helpful hint I'd like to pass along—they can be largely eliminated with, of all things, Visine eye drops.

The porn industry has played an important part in shaping pubic styles. Jordan Stein writes in an article titled "Has Porn Gone Mainstream?": "Consider the near icon status the female porn star has achieved. She is so mainstream that even good girls are imitating her various styles of undress, disappearing hair and all. Porn chic? You bet."

However, Julia Baird writes in *Celebrity Porn*: "The idea that the fashion industry can strip, then exhibit women in the name of 'porn chic' is a bit silly, frankly. But, 'flesh is the new fabric' could be the new catchcry. Americans call their bush George W. It's fashionable—the curious fact is that it is fueled by the porn aesthetic that celebrities love to love."

Among Hollywood actresses, Gwyneth Paltrow and Kirstie Alley have both admitted favoring Brazilian wax jobs, where most of their pubic hair is removed, leaving a small tuft that remains hidden under a thong bikini. Sarah Jessica Parker's character, Carrie Bradshaw, had her pubic hair removed during the third season of *Sex and the City*. Presumably, it's now in the Smithsonian museum along with Archie Bunker's chair and the Fonz's jacket.

On ABC's *Women's Murder Club*, a medical examiner directs her gaze to the crotch of a female corpse and says, "That's not your mama's bikini wax." On *The View*, Joy Behar said, "No pubic hair creates a wind tunnel." And in a hysterical episode of HBO's dark comedy series, *Curb Your Enthusiasm*, former *Seinfeld* producer Larry David performed oral sex on his wife, and in the process he sort of swallowed one of her pubic hairs. The next day, he was still choking on it, like a cat trying to get rid of a hairball.

A psychologist at Harvard Medical School and author of *Survival of the Prettiest: The Science of Beauty*, Nancy Etcoff, writes that "There's also an erotic, sexual component to hairlessness because your skin is more sensitive when it's more exposed. Women today are emulating porn stars who have no pubic hair, and I think men like it."

My own resistance to the plethora of bald pussies stems from my preadolescent days when pubic hair was such a big taboo that I became obsessed with it. In those pre-bikini days, I would go to Coney Island and stroll around the sand, sneaking glances at ladies in the hope of finding a few stray curlicues of forbidden pubic hair peeking out from their various and sun-dried crotches. And if I was able to discover any, why, it felt as though I had experienced a really productive afternoon.

Betty Dodson, sex educator and producer of *Viva La Vulva*, says, "I think we have changing ideas about what's public and what's private. And now that nudity is more public—nude beaches, routine nudity in film, and the enormous amount of exhibitionism and porn on the Web—I'm not surprised to see a trend toward pubic shaving. I think it's probably here to stay."

As for men, California Governor and former actor Arnold Schwarzenegger was only joking when he announced that he was going to get a bikini wax, but actually, Beverly Hills skin care and waxing expert Nance Mitchell has about fifty regular male customers that come for pubic waxing who "are not gay and they are not porn stars. Some go totally bare, some just do the shaft and up around the pelvic area." She explains that "It depends on what their wives and girlfriends want. Men go along because removing the hair makes the whole package look bigger."

Yes, the *illusion* of size does matter.

THE TASTE OF SPERM

THE TASTE OF SPERM

Online sexology columnist Sandor Gardos was asked, "How do I increase the amount of my ejaculate? I've noticed porn stars seem to ejaculate copious amounts of fluid, and I'd like to be able to wow my partner." Dr. Gardos points out that "the actors in porn films are professionals. Even they often don't ejaculate that much—sometimes movie makers will supplement with synthetic semen shot from a small tube."

Well, I'm just shocked to realize that somewhere in America there must be a group of scientists in a laboratory who earn their salaries by manufacturing fake semen.

Meanwhile, ManNotIncluded.com has become the first cyberspace sperm bank for lesbians and single women who want to become pregnant. They are matched with anonymous donors who have the desired race, eye color, height and weight, then sent instructions on how to inseminate themselves. John

Gonzalez, founder of the website, hopes this service will over-come the hurdles presented by bureaucracies and fertility clinics who are prejudiced against same-sex couples.

"Lesbians hook up with gay men all the time," he says, "either friends or guys they've met through personal ads. We are now simply allowing them to do so safely and without discrimination."

On the other hand, in the movie, *Sarah Silverman: Jesus Is Magic*—a performance by one of the best and raunchiest female stand-up comedians—she describes a sure method of birth control: "coming all over her face." Of course, that punch line is derived from the ever popular image on Internet porn sites, where I look in vain for the small print with messages warning, "Do Not Try This Particular Money Shot At Home" and "This Is Not Exactly What She Means When She Says She'd Like To Get a Facial For Her Birthday."

Furthermore, in Chelsea, Michigan, Book Crafters has refused to print *Baboon Dooley, Rock Critic*, a collection of John Crawford's comic strip, because his protagonist accidentally drinks from a glass of semen. He spits it out upon learning the content, only to be called a sexist, and challenged: "You'd expect a *woman* to drink it, right?" However, on CNN, author Hugh Prather was a guest, and the subject was couples. A caller revealed his problem: "The trouble is, when I come in her mouth, she can't really swallow it all." The anchor quickly hung up on this premature ejaculation.

Cartoonist Mary Lawton depicted a character saying, "I just found out that alfalfa sprouts smell like sperm. Does this mean I should practice safe salad?" But humorist Jacqueline Shtuyote confides in me, "Sperm is basically tasteless. The truth should be out about this. Men seem to think that their white stuff is a culinary delight, yet I know of no culinary courses extolling the flavor of sperm. And if, as rumored, Jack in the Box cooks occasionally spill their cum on an irritating customer's hamburger, how many of us would be pleased with the added ingredient?

"Why can't we find something that changes the flavor of cum? Then men could squirt red stuff that is raspberry flavored, or brown stuff that is chocolate flavored. Shy women could finally delight in swallowing their lovers' cum. No sperm would ever be spit out again. There could be a pill to make cum taste like fast-food hamburgers. Maybe then we wouldn't mind if we found out that the secret sauce on top of Jack in the Box hamburgers is, after all, sperm."

But let's not forget those who don't eat meat. They face an ethical dilemma—whether or not it's an acceptable practice for a vegetarian to give a blow job, and if so, is it all right to swallow? The general practice is that, yes, it's definitely okay to give a blow job because no animal is harmed in the process. And, yes, it's also okay to ingest the sperm because it's a good source of protein, something that's often lacking when meat is removed from the diet.

Finally—and this could possibly be an urban legend—in a biology class at Harvard University, a professor was discussing the high glucose levels found in semen which give the sperm all that energy for their journey. A female freshman raised her hand and asked, "If I understand you correctly, you're saying there is a lot of glucose, as in sugar, in semen?"

"That's correct," replied the professor. The student asked,

"Then why doesn't it taste sweet?"

"It doesn't taste sweet," he answered as she realized what her question implied. She blushed, picked up her books and headed for the door as he continued, "because the taste buds for sweetness are on the tip of your tongue and not the back of your throat. Have a good day."

DISINFORMATION PORN

DISINFORMATION PORN

This is the story behind the postings of a few chapters from *Trance Formation of America* that can now be found on the Internet. The book was written by Cathy O'Brien, who claims to be a victim of the CIA's MK-Ultra mind-control, child-sex-slave program, Project Monarch. Her husband, Mark Phillips, claims that, having worked for the CIA, where he learned hypnosis, he rescued Cathy, deprogrammed her and collaborated on their book.

At the age of thirteen, Cathy met the man "who would become my owner"—Senator Robert Byrd. "I undressed and climbed into his bed as ordered," she writes. "I was momentarily relieved to find that his penis was abnormally tiny—so small it didn't even hurt! And I could breathe with it in my mouth! Then he began to indulge himself in his brutal perversions. The spankings and police handcuffs I had previously endured were child's play compared to Senator Byrd's near-death tortures...."

Gerald Ford—"my first president"—also "brutally, sexually assaulted" her, as did Ford's chief of staff, Dick Cheney. After she was hunted down and caught in Cheney's game of "human hunting," she stood naked in his hunting lodge office as he paced around her and gave her this choice: "I could stuff you and mount you like a jackalope and call you a two-legged deer. Or I could stuff you with this [he unzipped his pants to reveal his oversized penis] right down your throat and then mount you. Which do you prefer?"

Apparently, Cheney's oversized penis balanced out Senator Byrd's undersized penis.

Cathy specialized in political figures (although she was also thrust upon by country singers such as "CIA operatives" Merle Haggard and Kris Kristofferson). Here's my favorite scene: "When Bill and Bob Bennett together sexually assaulted my daughter Kelly and me at the Bohemian Grove in 1986, I had already known Bill Bennett as a mind control programmer for some time. He apparently found perverse pleasure in whipping me...."

Cathy's first competitor was Brice Taylor, whose book is titled *Thanks for the Memories: The Memoirs of Bob Hope's and Henry Kissinger's Mind-Controlled Slave*. She asserts that Walt Disney raped her on Mr. Toad's Wild Ride, that she had sex with all three Kennedy brothers—plus JFK, Jr. when he was twelve—and has cavorted with public figures ranging from Prince Charles to Alan Greenspan, from Elvis Presley to Neil Diamond, from Johnny Carson to Ed McMahon, not to mention a threesome with her 13-year-old daughter, Kelly, and

Sylvester Stallone, who filmed them in *Dolphin Porn*, videos of dolphins penetrating women in the ocean.

"Perhaps there is a deeper conspiracy involved here," Robert Sterling, editor of an online publication, *The Konformist*, told me, "an attempt to discredit legitimate research into CIA dirty deeds. The most effective form of disinformation is that which blurs truth with fiction so effectively that they become impossible to differentiate. At the time Cathy O'Brien hit the lecture circuit, some powerful research was starting to circulate in alternative circles involving Satanic pedophilia operations. The end result of O'Brien's and Taylor's public ravings has been to trivialize this research by association. The CIA itself could be behind the plot. Both Cathy and Brice had the 'help' of self-described 'renegade CIA operatives' in the recovery of their memories. It's quite possible those operatives weren't renegades. Their help might have involved implanting bogus tales."

Remember when the Bush administration announced that there would be an Office of Disinformation—and then, as its first official act, the Office of Disinformation announced that there would *not* be an Office of Disinformation after all? And now there's disinformation porn.

Cathy O'Brien's book has sold over 20,000 copies. Her following is heavily right-wing Christians and patriot groups. An online review posted by Jaye Beldo suggested "grabbing a copy of *Trance Formation of America* and heading to the nearest bathroom with a jar of Vaseline. Why not infuse new life into your worn-out sexual fantasies by envisioning some of the scenes spelled out in Cathy O'Brien's supposed exposé of the pedophile shenanigans of our government officials? I mean, how could you not get excited over picturing Hillary Clinton going down on the author's deformed vagina like a starved wolf?"

Mark Phillips responded with a threatening e-mail to Beldo because he had attacked the book's "integrity." The irony is that if you surf the Web, under the category of bondage you will eventually come across those chapters downloaded from *Trance Formation of America*.

HOBO SEX AND
CRACK WHORE CONFESSIONS

HOBO SEX AND CRACK WHORE CONFESSIONS

When I was a kid, I wanted to be a hobo. It seemed like an exciting life, fueled by freedom. Of course, grown-ups tried to discourage me. They thought I wanted to be a bum. I wasn't interested in panhandling, though. I just figured that it would be fun to travel in a boxcar, visit different cities, cook my mulligan stew—whatever *that* is—over a campfire and sleep outdoors under the stars. In my mind, it was a romantic fantasy, not something I planned to do in order to make all my relatives feel ashamed. I even subscribed to the *Hobo News*.

I was reminded of this recently when I read about the death of Maurice "Steam Train Maury" Graham at the age of 89. In hobo jargon, he "caught the west-bound train." Graham began hopping freights when he was only fourteen years old. At the National Hobo Convention in 2004, he was anointed Grand Patriarch of the Hobos. He once said, "A hobo is just a guy who went camping and never came home." In his book, *Tales of the Iron Road: My Life as King of the Hobos*, published in 1990, he described how such a carefree lifestyle has changed:

"It used to be that a hobo had to be a good naturalist—he had to know all the roots, berries, grasses and weeds that are edible, and how to catch small game without weapons and how to be a good fisherman. But to survive as a hobo today, you practically have to be a pharmacist. They're hauling things in freight trains, like chemicals and pesticides that weren't even invented five years ago."

Since then, boxcars have been sealed, and the prosecution of trespassers has been intensified. But, from my adolescent days, I've wondered about the sex lives of hobos. There was something both glamorous and unattractive about them, something both exciting and unappetizing, as revealed in the media. The *New York Times* obituary repeated Graham's story of the Pennsylvania Kid, who shaved with a piece of glass from a Coke bottle. When the *Washington Post* asked him if it was true that some hobos used deodorant, he replied, "It's a shame, but I don't know what we can do about it." And the *Los Angeles Times* review of his book wondered if it neglected "a darker, hard-drinking, womanizing, gambling side" of his nature.

Do modern hobos have access to the Internet, and if so, is there online porn available for them? *Seattle Weekly* sex columnist, Judy "Bad Advice" McGuire, published a reader's question: "You once wrote that there is 'nothing that doesn't get somebody off.' What about poverty? I searched Google for pornography depicting the homeless or otherwise poverty-ridden as objects of lust, and found nothing. Oh, and just to clarify, I found nothing depicting poor, foul-smelling bums and bag ladies as objects of lust. I found a few sites that specialized in homeless gay men, but these men were hygienic, in decent shape, and they were not portrayed in a poverty-stricken environment or state."

"It's days like these," McGuire responded, "when I find myself typing in phrases like 'foxy naked homeless ladies' into assorted search engines, that I really start to wonder about my life choices. But let's get down to the business at hand. As there are folks who consider dining on feces the ultimate erotic experience and still others who get off on jamming metal rods up their urethras, it's hardly shocking that there are those who find the desperately poor and/or hopelessly (and homelessly) drug-addicted wank-worthy. Sigh. Don't these tragic types have enough problems without being turned into fodder for some control freak's masturbatory fantasies?" But she did discover "one of the more 'authentic' sites"—hobosexual.com—which I checked out and linked on to several "Hobofoot" websites.

Boss Trucker: "Galleries feature mature, old school drivers in the buff. The men shown in Hobofoot websites are older, seasoned men. And before anybody gets their panties in a bunch, we do not place truckers and hobos in the same category. The majority of truckers we meet are *very* clean, professional men."

Black Eye Saloon: "This is the first gallery originally called 'Hoboboot.' This unique website features *real* hobos, veteran rail riders, hardened, modern day pirates and attractive road tramps…. Hi-res photos so close you can almost smell 'em."

Tough Nuts: "More old outlaws and drifter types spread out nekkid for the connoisseur."

Smegmen: "The latest website added to the Hobofoot web. More hi-res images of naked old tramps and rough cut vagabonds, close enough to breathe deep."

Silver Whisker Saloon: "Eighteen galleries of senior men 50+, bare buck nekkid and in living color. Handsome, naked old cowboys and silver daddies."

Rough Trade Male: "The best collection of older, hard black men online. Raunchy sex, body worship, full sexual servitude of ebony masters."

Sgt. Daddy's Men: "A big ass picture of older men, bears and masculine senior men."

I had started out wanting to satisfy my curiosity about the sex life of a hobo, and I ended up being reminded of the law of supply and demand. These characters weren't exactly what I was searching for. As Judy McGuire informed her reader, Hobosexual "didn't have the hygienic, muscular hotties you describe. [Those] peppering this site were on the opposite end of the spectrum from the soot-smudged pretty boys you discovered. These guys appeared to be the real deal: of a certain age (though hard living can age a fella, so who knows), sporting crusty rolls of fat and unkempt clumps of back hair (no manscaping here!). Obviously my computer doesn't come equipped with odorama, but if looks could smell, I'm willing to bet their aroma was fairly funkified.

"Since I didn't see any poverty-stricken pussy on any of the site's free pages (and wasn't about to enter my credit card info to dig deeper), I'm assuming this particular site caters to men who love men. So I set out to find something for the straight boys. Not shockingly, I couldn't find a single example of this smut geared toward women, straight or gay. (Probably because most of us have already dated musicians.) I thought I'd hit pay dirt when I stumbled across a calendar featuring homeless dames, but it turned out to be a charity project for some church. (Save yourself the trouble—the ladies depicted were all fully clothed.) Most of what I was able to track down for the het set featured some variation on the 'crack ho.' Apparently skeletal broads with missing teeth and a penchant for anal are a niche market I hadn't really been aware of. According to the website crackwhore-confessions.com, Linda, a self-professed proponent of the 'stem fast diet,' will 'toss your salad, croutons and all.' Yum."

So naturally I checked out that site, and found a whole slew of slovenly sluts, including:

*A lesbian who "used to double team the Johns with her girlfriend to make the good money. While hooking she has met her share of twisted guys. Once a guy paid her $50 to chew his cock like bubble gum until he came!"

*An 18-year-old who "tells all about the sickest requests of her dates, like a guy that has her step on his balls with high heels!"

*Chris, who "has the honor of being the only crack whore that was featured on *America's Most Wanted* and captured. In prison she learned how to make improvised strap-on dildos from her bull dyke cell mate."

*Miss Kitty, the Madame to a ring of crack whores, shares "some shocking stories, like the airline pilot that got strung out with her before his flights. She became a famous crack whore by making the news when she was busted with a politician!"

*Kimmy, who "has refined her oral skills from years of experience turning tricks on the street. She is so confident in her abilities to suck off a guy that she offers a money back guarantee!"

In their worst nightmares, not one of these poor souls had ever dreamed of becoming a crack whore, and their apparently genuine confessions are consistently and tragicomically poignant, ranging from a former beauty queen—whose escorting business backfired when her common-law husband became her employees' best paying customer, and now she's fighting for custody of her two children—to Sammi, whose "own mother turned her on to the street life, causing her to lose custody of her children, and then her husband left her for another man with no legs and a piss sack!"

But here may be the most heartbreaking story of all: "Karen has pneumonia and is 8 months pregnant. She wanted dope so bad that she refused medical attention to hit the streets to score. She is a total junkie, addicted to crack *and* heroin. Karen is a full service whore, taking it in all three holes. The grand finale is her sucking the ass juice off my cock! It's the first time I got a pregnant chick in the butt." Yes, after a question-and-answer session, the anonymous interviewer *does* have sex with the crack whore. The interviewer of Louise reveals that, "She started by giving me head, but she was so lazy that a $5 upgrade got me pussy."

The women also get paid for being interviewed. The interviewer promoting Patty describes her as "a veteran crack ho, who has an insatiable oral fixation and cum is a nutritional part of her daily diet. She has been known to suck off up to 30 guys a day to keep money in her pocket. Watch this video to hear her horrid tales of street walking in the concrete jungle. This crack whore was thrilled to do this video for only $20 and a hot lunch."

Judy McGuire writes: "I'm not at all surprised that there's a market for this brand of depravity. It's about control and power—a bit like bondage and sado-masochism, but with a class/socio-economic element that takes things to a completely different level. There's no 'safe word' when you're dealing with someone who's trapped in an alley and is weak from hunger, shaking from the cold, or sick because she desperately needs to fix herself. It's the ultimate power play. In fact, I'm a little shocked it's not more popular. So while I don't think there are many among us who would find actually being penniless and living on the streets very gratifying (there but for the grace of a rent-stabilized apartment go I), there are plenty who find having the upper hand the ultimate aphrodisiac."

No matter what turns on any individual porn seeker, there will always be a perfect mate patiently waiting to satisfy him on the Internet.

EATING SHIT
FOR FUN AND PROFIT

EATING SHIT FOR FUN AND PROFIT

I am in complete awe of the democracy of the Internet, which presents an infinite menu for individual tastes and ideologies, and in this context, specifically to viewers of online porn. From golden showers to ejaculating females, from gay hunks to glittery she-males, the World Wide Web caters to virtually every imaginable kinky desire. With the privacy provided by a computer screen, you can easily worship at the fetish of your choice. But, in the process of surfing porn sites—for research purposes only, of course—I realized that I had never come across a site specializing in coprophagia. It means eating shit. Literally.

There's an old saying among nutritionists: "You are what you eat." However, comedian Darryl Henriques, playing the role of a New Age swami, says, "You are what you don't shit."

One of the nastiest things you can say to someone is, "Eat shit." A nonfiction book, *The Pit*, revealed a strange cult in San

Francisco where a group of successful businessmen were forced, along with other acts of humiliation, to eat their own shit. Ultimately, they were represented in a lawsuit by flamboyant attorney Melvin Belli.

In 2007, the *Rhode Island Journal* reported that a former inmate at the Adult Correctional Institution in Providence "who accused a guard of forcing him to taste his own feces... has accepted a $120,000 settlement from the state." The guard was being prosecuted for striking him in the head with a telephone book. "The incident involving the fecal matter is not a crime and he cannot be prosecuted for that." And *Prison Legal News* reported "a case out of Texas where a federal judge held that guards putting their feces in a prisoner's food occasionally was not unconstitutional and he likened it to finding pebbles in beans."

But those are all examples of involuntary shit eating, and what we're talking about here is the voluntary kind. For many years I heard stories that comic actor Danny Thomas, the star of *Make Room For Daddy*, was a coprophagiac. The reference was even infiltrated into a roast of Chevy Chase. "How about that new *Saturday Night Live* book," said musician Paul Shaffer. "They were pretty rough on Chevy. I haven't seen anybody eat that much shit since the biography of Danny Thomas."

I had assumed that this was all just another urban legend until I bumped into an old friend who was now working as a call girl in Hollywood. Over lunch, she mentioned the names of some of her celebrity clients, including Danny Thomas. She told me how he had hired her to save her solid waste in her panties so that he could rub the panties on his face and gobble up her shit as though it were cotton candy.

When he finished, he would wash himself thoroughly, then pay her, and, as if coming out of a trance, he'd say, "Where was I?" He was trying to distance himself from what he had just done. Instant denial. Since then, I have believed that Danny Thomas's fundraising for Saint Jude's Hospital was really for the purpose of having secret access to their used bedpans.

Anyway, I googled "Eating Shit." Topping the list was "Shit Eating Grins: In Defense of Adam Sandler, *South Park* and the Proud Tradition of Poop Humor"—an article in Salon.com. But sure enough, I was soon led to hard-core shit-eating sites, which I found totally disgusting yet absolutely riveting. You may not want to read any further, but we both know you will.

There are photos of beautiful women shitting; if you click for a close-up you can spot a yellow kernel of corn in one big brown chunk-o'-shit. Women are spreading shit all over their naked bodies and inside their vaginas. A pair of lovely lesbians are eating handfuls of shit, then tongue kissing each other. Two women are eating the same lengthy turd, starting from opposite ends. A woman, fully dressed, wearing a mini-skirt, is shitting as she walks along the sidewalk. One woman is shitting into another woman's mouth. Mmmm, good to the last dingleberry.

Among the shit-eating sites, there are Asian movies. Here's a couple of descriptions: "A bunch of kinky Japanese guys find some truly hot looking girls and take them down below the streets of Tokyo into a real sewer full of shit." And, "Cute Kyoko's diarrhea suddenly acts up again. Her piano teacher becomes a willing student of hot scat games. Lots of shit pours out of her hot ass into his waiting mouth. Then she asks if he would rub it all over her. Sure, why not, he says."

If there is one particular image that remains in my mind's eye, it is of an innocent looking, attractive teenager—she's over eighteen, of course—and she is cheerfully drinking a shit-shake through a straw from an old-fashioned malted milk glass.

I thought about her father discovering that photo in cyber-space, yet he is unable to confront his daughter about it because he would then have to admit what *he* was doing at that site. I mean, this isn't exactly the type of thing that would be mass e-mailed by one of those selfless spammers. And even if the father did confess to his daughter, he would undoubtedly hesitate to ask if he could eat *her* shit, because that could be considered a form of incest, and you have to draw the line somewhere, right?

There must be an especially strong bond among copropha-giacs, though, because they have experienced in common a form of liberation from a taboo that can be traced all the way back to infancy, when a parent would cringe and say, "Stop! Don't eat that! I said *no*!"

Who knows, some day coprophagia might even become a religion?

Holy shit!

PORN DOGS

PORN DOGS

Andrea Nemerson, who writes an alternate sex column for the *San Francisco Bay Guardian*, published this letter from a reader: "I know this woman, and she has a fetish with bringing dead animals into the bedroom. She likes to dress up in a pink bunny suit and hop around. Then, with the dead animals, she tries to insert them anally. She tickles her cooch with the animals' tails and then cuts them open and feeds on the spleen and liver."

Okay, that particular letter turned out to be a hoax. Nevertheless, bestiality fetishes have become quite chic these days. There are websites that feature "slutty chicks" fondling, fucking and sucking horses, snakes, cows, dogs, monkeys, sheep, donkeys, goats, pigs, and occasionally necking with a giraffe or humping a camel. Unlike regular commercial movies shown in theaters, Internet porn doesn't include any such disclaimers as "No animals were harmed during the making of this film."

There are no overseers from the American Humane Society. Nor are there any complaints from PETA (People For the Ethical Treatment of Animals).

But in Japan, when it comes to professional porn animals, it's a different story, or rather, let's say it's a horse of another color. In fact, many Japanese porn actresses have been complaining that they only make half the wages of their canine co-stars, who acquire an average of 200,000 yen per movie. In America, an owner might get paid off, but the animals themselves earn nothing except maybe a few extra Dog Yummies.

In Japan, the so-called Butter Dogs are very popular. That name is derived from the spreading of butter on the labia of their mistresses before the great licking scenes. One porn flick, *Butter Dog Story DX*, featured a dog performing orally on eight women. Labrador Retrievers are a favorite because of their obedient nature and their popularity throughout Japan.

"It is not like we breed them to be Butter Dogs," explained a spokesperson for Alpha International, the company that produced *Butter Dog Story DX*. "We mostly use dogs from canine talent agencies. We have to have dogs that are used to being around humans, as well as movie studios. By the way, it is not butter that we lather over the women any more, either. We use non-sugar yogurt. When we used butter, the dogs ended up getting too fat, and we were worried about their health."

Since few canine talent agencies want to have their clients appear in bestiality movies, producers have to exploit personal contacts in order to get the dog trainers to cooperate. According to an official at one Japanese canine talent agency, "There is no real special training for the Butter Dogs. The most important thing is their nature. Basically, we want dogs that are friendly toward humans and that are obedient. It's important that they don't bark. We do train them not to bark unnecessarily. We also teach them not to bark if they're touched by somebody other than their trainer. These conditions do not apply just for the adult movie world, but for any dog that's going to appear on screen."

Japan's most prolific director of bestiality movies, Sukeo Yamane, points out that Butter Dogs pose certain production problems. "It's only natural," he says, "that everybody is a bit worried about diseases when it comes to dogs, even if they're pets. But I've never experienced any sort of illness related problems. Trainers would make sure they never delivered us an infected dog. In fact, trainers are more likely to be worried if the actresses have got a venereal disease. You hear stories of actors being infected by actresses. That's why we always make sure we only choose girls who are clean. Unlike humans, you can't put a condom on the dogs because they hate them."

It has been determined—and believe me, I have no idea *how* it was determined—that dogs' lives are shortened if they ejaculate too many times. Labrador Retrievers usually live for about ten years, but if they've appeared in porn flicks (in which dogs are legally allowed to be under eighteen years old), their lifespan is generally cut in half. That's why responsible canine talent agencies insist that their dogs be permitted to ejaculate only once per day while shooting a porn flick. "Sometimes," admitted one director, "it takes a full day to do a shoot. Just like humans, dogs aren't always able to rise when they want to, so we can be stuck around waiting for hours at a time until the pooch is properly aroused. It's hard to arouse a dog when it's not in heat. That is why we sometimes start a shoot early in the morning and do not finish it until the middle of the night."

But, hey, wouldn't you think that they'd have available on the set a fluffer for Fluffy?

"I FUCK DEAD PEOPLE"

"I FUCK DEAD PEOPLE"

You don't see any porn sites that feature intercourse with corpses, and if you do, how do you know they're really dead? But, say what you will about California Governor Arnold Schwarzenegger, you have to give him credit for signing a bill to forbid necrophilia. Under the new law, sex with a corpse is now a felony punishable by up to eight years in prison.

Age is no barrier. The state's first attempt to outlaw necrophilia—in response to a case of a man charged with having sex with the corpse of a four-year-old girl in Southern California—stalled in a legislative committee, but the bill was revived after an unsuccessful prosecution of a man who was found in a San Francisco funeral home, passed out on top of an elderly woman's corpse.

Necrophiliacs have been getting away with it all this time, but district attorneys will no longer be stymied by the lack of an official ban. According to Tyler Ochoa, a professor at Santa

Clara University of Law who has studied California cases involving allegations of necrophilia, "Prosecutors didn't have anything to charge these people with other than breaking and entering. But if they worked in a mortuary in the first place, prosecutors couldn't even charge them with that."

Whether necrophilia is a victimless crime may still be open to debate. Nevertheless, claiming that the act was consensual will not be considered as a legal defense. It should be noted that the necrophilia community ranges from those who are monogamous and stick with one partner for a lifetime, to those who are promiscuous and hop from casket to casket.

According to his own journal entry, Ralph Waldo Emerson, one of the most revered figures in American literary history, was so devastated by the death of his young wife, Ellen, that, shortly after her burial, he went out to the cemetery one night and dug up her corpse, though he didn't mention exactly what he did with it.

One of the most popular episodes of the police TV show, *Homicide: Life On the Street*, was about the investigation of an old lonely widower, a mortician, who used to party with the corpses, setting them around a table as if they were alive. The police investigated him because he shot a neighbor who knew about this practice, and then sat in the garden and waited for the cops. But again, the mortician's relationship with those corpses may have been purely platonic.

Let us now eavesdrop on the dialogue of a few participants in an Internet support group, Necrophiliacs Anonymous:

"Obviously, neither a corpse nor a four-year-old can provide consent, but if you leave permission in your will for your lonesome spouse or significant other to have one last fling with your mortal coil, shouldn't the state of California respect your wishes?"

"I still think that organ donation is a better cause. It's just that I believe the only offense here is really violation of private property. I wonder if someone gives their partner, in a will, the right to have sex with their body after their death, will it be legal?"

"Or, even without that permission, if you are an only heir of somebody, doesn't it mean their body belongs to you? It sounds gross, but isn't it an issue of private rights in the United States of America, that likes so much the idea of individualism and is ready to exploit people and the environment in the name of that ideal?"

"I never understood why people think that having sex with a dead body is worse than raping a living person. To me, that's the worst kind, and then raping poor helpless animals. I really couldn't care less about my *own* dead body."

Conversely, the late evangelist turned comedian, Sam Kinison, had a great routine about necrophilia: "Well, that's it, man—I'm dead. Nothing else bad can happen to me now. Wait a minute—what's that? What's this guy doing? What's going on here? [Screams] Oh oh oh oh oh OH OH OH OH OH *OOOOOOHHHHHH NOOOOOOO!!! Live in Hell!!!*"

The majority of cannibalistic serial killers are motivated by a kind of necrophilia—it's usually a highly sexually arousing experience for them when they eat their victims. Here, from my "Great Moments in Necrophila" file, is a dispatch from the Associated Press:

"The prosecution in the insanity trial of serial killer Jeffrey Dahmer rested its case. Dahmer has confessed to killing and dismembering 17 young males since 1978. A jury must decide if he will be sent to prison or a mental institution. The final prosecution witness, Dr. Park Dietz, a psychiatrist, testified that Dahmer wore condoms when having sex with his dead victims, showing that he could control his urge to have intercourse with corpses."

I smell a public service announcement there: "If Jeffrey Dahmer is sane enough to have safe sex, what about *you*?"

PORN PROVIDES
PRODUCT PLACEMENT

PORN PROVIDES PRODUCT PLACEMENT

Of course it's tragic when *anybody* gets AIDS, but in the porn industry, when a couple of actors tested positive for HIV—then it was four, then it was six—various producers actually had to stop production while all their actors were getting tested. What you probably didn't know, though, is that in order to make up for the funds, which were lost during the delay, they decided that when they started producing again, their new features would garner extra income by including product placement.

"If it's good enough for *American Idol*," said one porn producer, referring to the mandatory drinking of Coca-Cola by the three judges on that show, "then it's good enough for us."

"How do you know that was product placement?" his partner asked. "You're just cynical. You probably think that Bob Dole got paid by the Paper Mate Pen company for always holding that pen in his crippled hand."

"No, I'm not *that* cynical," replied the first producer. "Dole fought in World War II, and a rocket launcher *embedded* that pen in his hand."

In any case, these producers became the first in the business to experiment with product placement for extra revenue.

A beautiful young woman is masturbating with a clearly labeled Hitachi Magic Wand.

"This vibrator is not just for my clit," she says to the camera between moans. "It can stimulate erogenous zones I didn't even know I had."

Thus was the ice broken. Another entrepreneur presented a muscular man using a feather duster to cover his cock and balls and asshole with edible honey dust powder. When his girlfriend gives him a combination blow job and rim job, the viewer can't help but notice a close-up of the popular Kama Sutra logo.

The CEO of NextMedium, which has launched a product placement marketplace called Embed, states that, "To date, product placement has been opportunistic and Rolodex based. Our goal is to establish brand integration as an ad category." To meet that goal, a product could be written—that is, entrenched—into a story line.

Along those lines, in order to give a particular scene a certain organic feel, where product placement must be integral to the plot, a porn director arranged for a couple to use a sex machine built for two, with the male playing the role of an activist salesman.

"This is the Televibe 8100," he explains to her as they proceed to undress. "It can be operated remotely either by telephone or over the Internet."

She asks, "How does it work?"

"Well, you just hook it right into the phone, and it's controlled by this keypad, no matter how far away from each other we are. We could be anywhere in the world. For now, I'll simply go into the other room. Here, I'll show you."

He puts a Foxy Lady vibrating pussy sleeve on his erect penis and goes into the other room. However, it doesn't work because the necessary four triple-A batteries were not included. They both have a hearty laugh over his mistake and then they just get in bed to fuck like mad in the good old-fashioned way.

A similar theme was developed in the porn equivalent of a Tupperware Party. A pair of lesbians have a go at it with the *Penthouse* Snap-On Strap-On. Then a group of women take turns dirty dancing on the Johnny Lonely stripper pole.

Indeed, another porn movie also manages to slip in a bit of educational dialogue. The girl is waiting in her home for the proverbial pizza delivery boy.

"Hi, honey," he says, "I know that you're at the height of fertility, so I brought your favorite Trojan, the one that has ribbing and a French tickler on the reservoir tip."

"Oh," she responds, "that's so thoughtful of you. But, you know, just to avoid any irritation, I have this bottle of Astro-glide lubricant."

And then, he says, "Listen, I'm going out of town for a week, but I also brought this Clone-a-Willy kit, so we can make an exact vibrating rubber copy of my dick for you to use while I'm away."

"Wow," she exclaims, stroking the real thing to nice, solid hardness. "This is really a very romantic gesture."

So, this porn producer asks his partner, "You think we can make a product placement deal with Rolex for our next fisting flick?"

"Nah, because it wouldn't be *visible*."

"It's visible if you wear it above your elbow."

ADDICTED TO PORN

ADDICTED TO PORN

In the same issue of *Rolling Stone* that rap star Kanye West posed on the cover as Jesus Christ with a crown of thorns circling his head, he admitted inside the magazine that he's addicted to pornography. Now, what *would* Jesus do? It gives new meaning to the Second Coming. In *Hooked*, a documentary by Todd Ahlberg, a gay interviewee says, "The Internet is the drive-through for sex.... A guy starts going online out of curiosity. Then he realizes how easy it is and then before long..." He goes on to describe his deep fear of being addicted to online sex.

Oprah Winfrey stated on her daytime TV program that "Pornography is the number one addiction" in the United States. She proceeded to warn her virtually all-female audience with a rhetorical question: "Could this be *your* husband?" Kirk Franklin, a Grammy-winning gospel singer and recovering porn addict, was a guest on that show. Oh, yes, and he also had a new album to promote. Another guest was Robert Weiss, a self-styled expert on addiction to pornography. He claimed that ten percent of the forty million online porn users are addicts.

Which exasperated sex writer Susie Bright, who ranted on her website, susiebright.com:

"When will these people stop lying through their teeth? What an old phony Rob Weiss is! He's the original snake oil salesman. This hustler has made the rounds of TV talk shows for years, ranting about sex addiction. What about those figures he quotes about how many people 'watch' Internet porn, and how many are addicts? *He makes them up!* There's not a citation in the world to support him.

"He doesn't represent legitimate psychology in the slightest. In fact, every shrink I know recoils at his name. Weiss feeds off of all these hip new Christian fundamentalist churches. They 'use' porn to recruit. Without it, they're dead in the water. They play on people's sexual feelings to get them excited, and then shame the shit out of them. It is *so cruel* to lead them on and make them think they are dealing with a pathology that requires spending thousands of dollars to be cured by 'Doctor' Weiss."

Weiss is aided and abetted by Dear Abby and her fellow mainstream advice givers. Whenever they publish a column with a letter from an anxious wife or girlfriend who has discovered porn on her husband's or boyfriend's computer, the answer always assumes it's another case of addiction to porn and recommends that the poor fellow needs to seek professional help or else their marriage or their relationship will be doomed. It's not porn's fault, though.

An article in *the Los Angeles Times* stated: "If there is one psychological element that unites them, clinicians who work with these addicts say, it is a basic way to cope with depression or anxiety that rules the rest of their lives. Web porn becomes a kind of self-administered shock therapy." Fortunately, there are several support groups available, porn equivalents of Alcoholics Anonymous.

Let's look in on a typical meeting at Porn Anonymous:

"Hi, I'm Tom."

Everybody: "Hi, Tom."

"I'm here because I'm addicted to porn. Or at least my wife *thinks* I am. She caught me masturbating to my computer and she went berserk. She insisted that I attend Porn Anonymous, so here I am. But it's all her fault. She won't allow me to come on her face. I tried it once, and I'll never forget her scream: '*Do not ever ejaculate on my face again!*' Well, if I couldn't do it, at least I could watch somebody else doing it to get myself aroused. But the porn stars always look like *they're* really enjoying it, so I just assumed my wife would too...."

"Hi, my name is Dick."

"Hi, Dick."

"I'm a porn addict. It's no big deal to me. Porn, you know, I can take it or leave it. But I'd rather take it. That simple. But my girlfriend is jealous of my computer screen. She says, 'What, I'm not enough for you? Just because one time I said no, I was too tired.' I tell her, 'Look, it has nothing to do with you. I like to whack off and not worry about getting you off.' And we got into a big fight. She's yelling, 'Worry! You *worry* about getting me off? It's supposed to give you goddam pleasure!' Anyway, I promised her I would come here. I'm not ready to break off with her yet...."

"Hey, I'm Harry."

"Hey, Harry."

"Nobody had to tell me to come here. I know I'm a porn addict. Well, not exactly. I'm a porn-*addict* addict. I come here because the stories that porn addicts tell get me fuckin' horny. Then I go home and jerk off...."

THE GOVERNOR, THE HOOKER
AND THE PORN STAR

THE GOVERNOR, THE HOOKER AND THE PORN STAR

If former New York Governor Eliot Spitzer had only indulged in an affair with that woman, "Karen," he would not have been charged with a crime. However, in a bizarre spin of capitalist theory, the fact that he actually *paid* for her services—whether it was $50 or $5,000 makes no difference—he could conceivably be sent to prison, not for fucking her, but rather for *paying* his debt to her.

Had it been a romantic date rather than a business transaction, it would have been perfectly legal for him to present her with a costly piece of jewelry, take her out to a gourmet dinner, followed by a high priced Broadway play on opening night, and *then* when he proceeded to fuck her, he would not have been busted for committing the victimless crime of renting a female body for the evening.

Usually, it has been the chintzy street whore or the expensive call girl who gets arrested, not her client, but this was quite an unusual case. In the same hotel room in Washington D.C. that Spitzer would be spritzing around with Karen, he had just written, in an opinion piece for the *Washington Post* about the sub-prime loan tragedy: "Not only did the Bush administration do nothing to protect consumers, it embarked on an aggressive and unprecedented campaign to prevent states from protecting their residents from the very problems to which the federal government was turning a blind eye."

In fact, the reason Spitzer had flown to Washington was to launch a campaign to attack the arrogant Bush cabal and the arrogant corporations that empower them. He wrote, "When history tells the story of the sub-prime lending crisis and recounts the devastating effects on the lives of so many innocent home-owners, the Bush administration will not be judged favorably." Thus, the *real* motivation for Spitzer's arrest.

But let us flash back to 1974. My friend Margo St. James— who once masturbated me in a porn theater while wearing a nun's costume—organized the first Hookers Ball, which became an annual event. She founded the legendary prostitutes' rights organization, COYOTE (Call Off Your Old Tired Ethics), the purpose of which has evolved into the celebration a few months ago of International Sex Worker Rights Day, an unofficial holiday that originated in 2001 when over 25,000 sex workers gathered in India for such a festival.

Because critics of the porn industry have equated the actresses in adult movies with prostitutes because they both get paid for having sex, I thought it would be appropriate now to seek Margo's take on that particular phenomenon. She was, after all, a pioneer activist in the field of sex workers.

"The Internet porn industry seems to be made up of amateurs," she told me, "but the topic serves well as advertising for the real thing. Porn was legalized by case law. Although it fits the description of sex work, it is usually operated by third parties, mostly men. This seemed okay, because there isn't sex between two parties for money. Though there are many people having sex together for the cameras, the porn actors are paid by a third party.

"Legalization of sex work in the *de facto* way our culture has developed it—under the heading of 'massage,' 'escort,' and so forth—keeps the illusion alive that women aren't doing it for the money directly. So when we discussed the issue at our conventions, we felt that actual legalization would simply make the government the pimp. Decriminalization, on the other hand, would respect the nature of sex, that of a cottage industry, leaving the money in the hands of the provider.

"The prostitution prohibition criminalizes women for the money, not the sex. The law is clear that adults in private can have all the sex they think they want as long as no consideration is offered or accepted. This is the foundation for keeping women's bodies firmly in the control of the government as far as their sexuality and right to choose to have children. As long as this stigma is placed on women, Roe vs. Wade is on shaky ground. This is the bottom line for women's rights, and repeal is imperative for full equality."

I have always thought that prostitutes were on the front lines of the women's movement. For, as long as the police can harass a woman on the street because she merely *looks* like a hooker, they can hassle *any* woman on the street. Ultimately, because of what Margo St. James refers to as "prostitution prohibition," Eliot Spitzer has most likely lost forever his ambition of becoming president of the United States. As for his one-night stand, Karen, she will probably get her own talk show on HBO, or maybe even the Oxygen channel.

A LETTER TO "JUDGE PORN"

A LETTER TO "JUDGE PORN"

Dear Judge Porn,

I know your name is actually Alex Kozinski, but I couldn't resist asking this rhetorical question: Should Judge Porn judge porn? Specifically, in your capacity as chief justice of the 9th Circuit Court of Appeals, you were given the case of Ira Isaacs, a producer and distributor of pornography. His defense is that the movies he sells are works of art and are therefore protected by the First Amendment.

As you must know, the U.S. Department of Justice Obscenity Task Force, which was formed in 2005 after Christian conservative groups pressured the Bush administration to crack down on porn, is "dedicated exclusively to the protection of America's children and families through enforcement of obscenity laws." The task force has won convictions in more than a dozen cases—five in Texas alone—and they've won mostly on the basis of plea bargains. But, rather than go after the makers of plain vanilla porn, these prosecutors focus on fetishes because a jury is more likely to find guilty a defendant who is responsible for porn flicks that feature defecation and sex with animals. Which of course brings up another rhetorical question: "Who's to say what art is?"

And so, Judge Porn, when jury selection began, you urged potential jurors to be open about their opinions. In the first hour, you dismissed 26 men and women who acknowledged that they could not be fair to defendant Isaacs because they were so repulsed by the subject matter of his products. At the end of the first day, from a panel of 100, half were excused. Isaacs himself admitted, "I think I'd freak out if I had to watch six hours of the stuff." And then the god of Irony descended upon you. On a section of *your own* website that you mistakenly considered to be private, a Beverly Hills attorney—in the midst of a dispute with you about another matter—was able to find questionable material and download it on a CD, including:

A slide show strip-tease starring a transsexual. A slide show, "BrazilianHairCut," depicting a vagina being shaved. A close-up of a shaved crotch with the caption, "Democrats New Slogan— Read My Lips—No More Bush." A parody of the MasterCard commercial, depicting four women smiling for the camera, but one of them has her skirt hiked up far enough to reveal her pubic hair, accompanied by a punchline, "Your Beaver on the Internet: Priceless." A foreign commercial in which a woman rolls a cigar between her bare breasts (shades of Bill Clinton). A German commercial, "Nutcracker," in which a woman emerges from a shower, approaches a plate of walnuts, and cracks them by placing them between her buttocks and squeezing (shades of the Hillary Clinton nutcracker). "HomerLookAlike," with the face of Homer Simpson superimposed on a vagina. A half-dressed man cavorting with a sexually aroused farm animal.

Photos of naked women on all fours painted to look like cows. A folder of "camel toe" photos with close-ups of female crotches in snug-fitting panties (no more obscene than similar images in a mainstream movie, "The Weather Man"). A woman in a shower massaging her breasts, each of which is larger than her head. A video, "Upside Down," presenting a contortionist couple performing oral sex on each other. A parody of a video, "BestWomanDriver," of a woman who, while driving a car, gives a male passenger a hand job until he comes on her hand, and then she licks her fingers—all of which certainly seems safer than driving while text messaging. A video, "ChineseMassProduction," showing more than a hundred naked Asian couples simultaneously fucking in the exact same position. Plus urination, defecation—but not in a sexual context—and bestiality. Plus the only video which really got me aroused—a dog that can play Ping-Pong with his tail.

Well, Judge, you had to drop out of the Isaacs case and declare a mistrial. Not that you had necessarily violated the law. It's just that your collection could be perceived as tainting your decisions in the Isaacs case. What's more, it could conceivably spoil your chance to ever be appointed to the U.S. Supreme Court. And that makes me sad, because you are known as a strong defender of free speech.

It was poignant the way your wife came to your aid, though. "Alex is not into porn," she stated in a 2,000-word defense of you on her own website, "he is into funny—and sometimes funny has a sexual character." Yet another rhetorical question: Who's to say what's funny? May I suggest a game that's going around which the two of you might enjoy sharing with guests at your next dinner party. It's easy to play. All you do is take the name of your first pet and then the name of the first street you lived on, and the result will be your very own porn name.

Sincerely,
Skippy Broadway

WOMEN AND PORN

WOMEN AND PORN

Along with everything else, the marketing of porn continues to evolve. In the course of an interview with Susie Bright—whose latest anthology is *X: The Erotic Treasury*—I asked, "What aspect of online porn do you like?"

"The democratic nature of it," she replied, "that you can search and you shall find. That its basis was all free, a free exchange. That it brought such authentic, first-person networking and connection with it. Before the commercialization of online porn, there were years and infinite relationships and conversations that had built up. This was before 'spam' was something besides a Hawaiian loaf with cloves."

"And what aspect of online porn do you dislike?"

"The con job of it, like everywhere else. The dominance of big, boring, uncreative monoliths like the rest of mainstream entertainment. Blech."

But adult films aren't just for men any more. That's so 1970s. One survey showed that about 16% of men who have access to the Internet at work acknowledged having seen porn while on the job. Eight percent of women said they had. Another survey indicated that 20% of men and 13% of women watch porn at work.

And what about the women who produce porn? Writer/director Candida Royalle confesses, "I have absolutely no time for my sex life any more—I'm just working too much—and I'm engaged." Certainly those who participated in an *AVN* panel about porn have a vested interest in it. Shirley Isaacson, co-creater of Impulse TV, used to be with the Spice Network, where subscribers viewing habits were monitored.

"After the kids went to school, the buys came in very heavily," she recalls. "Around noon they started coming in again. They stopped around four when the kids started coming home from school. So we *know* that women watch by themselves."

Carol Queen, staff sexologist at Good Vibrations, says, "Fifteen years ago you really had to give women a lot of encouragement. Today there is a sub-category of more diverse, sex-positive college-age women who wouldn't think twice about liking porn. Women would like to know just why these people are fucking. They often love that they're fucking, but they think that plot devices are fairly stupid, and they would like to see a little discernment in the way that the plot, if there is a plot at all, is set up."

Susie Bright adds, "Men wouldn't enjoy movies featuring men with limp dicks. Well, women don't like dry pussies either. They like to see women obviously getting off. I can't repeat that enough. What's funny to me are the producers who make hot stuff that women *would* like, who don't have a clue how to reach women about it. The production values [of female-ejaculation videos like *Cum Rain Cum Shine* and *Flower's Squirt Shower*] are terrible, the men are red-faced clowns, but the women's orgasmic raindown is irresistible. Every woman I know who sees them has to go excuse herself and beat off."

Susie has reported on her interview with porn director Tristan Taormino, whose *Ultimate Guide to Anal Sex for Women* won *AVN*'s "Best Anal Sex Release" award:

"Tristan has a knack for arguing with powerful men in the movie business. Spike Lee asked her to be his sex/dyke consultant for his movie, *She Hate Me*, a comedy about—among other things—predatory lesbians on the Baby-Making March. Spike would tell her things like, 'I really don't know any lesbians that well,' and then she'd look around at everyone who was working in his office and blink—'Hello! Are you blind?'

"He was flabbergasted at what she suggested, that vaginal orgasms are *not* the primary way women orgasm. She fought *sooooo* hard to get some realistic female sexiness in this movie, and after I saw the film, I was impressed with the battles she won and biting my lip at the ones she lost. Thank god she got a real vibrator in. She lost the strap-on dildo debate, though.

"But from a 'this-is-worth-noticing' perspective, the sheer numbers of black, Latin, Asian and biracial dykes in this film singlehandedly smashes the cliché that lesbian is for white college girls. There are so many heretofore 'unseen women' traipsing in and out of the sperm donor's apartment (this is the comedy part) that their very presence is inspiring."

On the *AVN* panel, Tristan said about porn flicks, "It's frustrating, because there's a segment of the industry that is still hanging on to the fact that only a tiny percentage of their customers are women and couples. I want to see people who clearly love sex, I want to see them having a good time. I want to see a lot of amazing real female orgasms. I want to see toys. I want to see vibrators."

According to historian Rachel Maines in *The Technology of Orgasm: "Hysteria," the Vibrator and Women's Sexual Satisfaction*, the vibrator was originally developed to perfect and automate a function that doctors had long performed for their female patients—the relief of physical, emotional and sexual tension through external pelvic massage, culminating in orgasm.

"Most of them did it," said Dr. Maines, "because they felt it was their duty. It wasn't sexual at all."

Which brings us to Sherri Williams, a casualty of the war on pleasure. She was acquitted of the heinous crime of selling non-prescription vibrators. She had violated an Alabama statute, which bans the sale of vibrators and other sex toys. The law prohibited "any device designed or marketed as useful primarily for the stimulation of human genital organs."

But the not-guilty verdict in her case was overturned by a 2-1 decision. In the Court of Appeals, the state's attorney general defended the statute, arguing that, "a ban on the sale of sexual devices and related orgasm-stimulating paraphernalia is rationally related to a legitimate interest in discouraging prurient interests in autonomous sex." Rationally related? Moreover, he said, "There is no constitutional right to purchase a product to use in pursuit of having an orgasm." There isn't?

Ironically, the FDA has approved a device specifically designed to help women achieve orgasm, marking the first time that the federal government has licensed an aid for women with sexual dysfunction. "The Eros," which uses the same basic principle as Viagra to promote sexual arousal—stimulating blood flow to the genital area—is a battery-operated vacuum attached to a suction cup that fits over the clitoris. The device, available only by prescription, costs $359. However, fingers, tongues and penises are all free. And still legal.

This country was founded by pioneers with a lust for freedom and by puritans with a disdain for pleasure. The problem is that those who are still burdened by that streak of anti-pleasure keep trying to impose unnecessary restrictive laws upon those who are pro-pleasure. What ever happened to "the pursuit of pleasure" mentioned in the preamble to the *Declaration of Independence*?

Ironically, journalist Gita Smith wrote in August 2007, "In Alabama, you can sell guns on any street corner but you can't sell sex toys. In other words, we are free to blow ourselves up at will. We just can't blow up a dolly with big red lips and openings in her lifelike vinyl self.

"Alabama is a vibrator-free state. Well, technically you can go across state lines and buy sex toys in Georgia and Tennessee and carry them home. Today, the U.S. Supreme Court has shown a gleam of interest in this controversial state law. At the very least, this case seems to be a restraint-of-trade case as much as anything else, since the devices are sold in all the neighboring states. I would like to be a fly on the wall when oral arguments are heard.

"*Justice Antonin Scalia*: You say that the sale of the Twizzler-Twister should be banned?

"*Alabama Guy*: Yes, Your Honor.

"*Justice Samuel Alito*: And the Buzzer-Master?

"*Alabama Guy*: Yes, that too.

"*Justice Clarence Thomas*: What about the Coke can with the fake pubic hair?

"*Alabama Guy*: That one doesn't vibrate, so that one's okay.

"There is, and always has been, a strong strain of paternalism among lawmakers down here. And that paternalistic attitude makes them believe that they are the keepers of the Moral Keys. Us wee folk need protecting from sexual pleasures derived from plastic thingies made in China."

But, on the first Monday of October 2007, the Supreme Court declined to hear a challenge to Alabama's ban on the sale of sex toys. A three-judge panel had upheld the guilty verdict of the appeals court on February 14. Happy Valentine's Day to the roots of fascism in the private parts of America.

Sherri Williams, who faces a $10,000 fine and one year of hard labor, called the Supreme Court's decision not to review the law "further evidence of religion in politics." She plans to sue again, this time on First Amendment free speech grounds.

"My motto," she says, "has been they are going to have to pry this vibrator from my cold, dead hand. I refuse to give up."

ABOUT THE AUTHOR

PAUL KRASSNER is the author of several books, a co-founder of the Yippies and publishes the Disneyland Memorial Orgy poster (available at www.paulkrassner.com). He edited the groundbreaking satirical magazine, *The Realist* (1958-2001), but when *People* magazine called him "father of the underground press," he immediately demanded a paternity test. He is a columnist for *AVN Online* and *High Times*, and the only person in the world ever to receive awards from both *Playboy* magazine (for humor) and the Feminist Party Media Workshop (for journalism). He has also received an ACLU Uppie (Upton Sinclair) Award for dedication to freedom of expression, and at the annual Cannabis Cup in Amsterdam he was inducted into the Counterculture Hall of Fame—"my ambition," Krassner claims, "since I was three years old."